Sing My Whole Life Long

Sing My Whole Life Long

Jenny Vincent's
Life in Folk Music
and Activism

CRAIG SMITH

FOREWORD BY RONALD D. COHEN

PREFACE BY JOHN NICHOLS

UNIVERSITY OF NEW MEXICO PRESS ALBUQUERQUE

12 11 10 09 08 07   1 2 3 4 5 6 7

LIBRARY OF CONGRESS CATALOGING-IN-PUBLICATION DATA

Smith, Craig, 1947 July 30–
Sing my whole life long : Jenny Vincent's life in folk music and activism /
Craig Smith ; foreword by Ronald D. Cohen ; preface by John Nichols.
p. cm. — (CounterCulture series)
Includes bibliographical references (p.   ) and index.
ISBN 978-0-8263-4226-3 (PBK. : ALK. PAPER)
1. Vincent, Jenny Wells. 2. Folk singers—United States—Biography.
3. Political activists—United States—Biography. I. Title.
ML420.V379S65   2006
782.42162'0092—dc22
[B]

2006101190

Book and cover design and
type composition by Kathleen Sparkes

This book is typeset using Sabon 11/14.5, 26P
Display type is Murray Hill

Contents

Foreword

Ronald D. Cohen

Craig Smith has written a fascinating account of the incredible life and times of Jenny Vincent. Spanning most of the twentieth century (and into the twenty-first), Jenny's life has connected with many remarkable and influential individuals and events, often through her musical life and talents. Music has played a vital role in political organizing on the left, which can be traced through Jenny's long life. Some background information is necessary in order to more fully understand this history.

Jenny's classical music training took a significant turn when she was exposed to the world's folk music at the North Shore Country Day School in 1926. Indeed, her musical career would be unique in that she specialized in non-English songs, particularly those in Spanish. Songs from around the world were not unusual in school and other songbooks beginning early in the century, but they were not particularly popular, except during the 1950s and again toward the end of the century. Indeed, what is known as "world music" has become widespread in recent decades, but this was not true for much of Jenny's life. So, while her musical life was rather untypical for a folk performer, she nonetheless also fit into a broad political left that included many fascinating individuals and events.

Along with her first husband, Dan Wells, Jenny was attracted to the Communist Party and the activities of the Old Left during the Depression. This was not unusual for intellectuals, artists, performers, labor activists, and numerous others who were appalled by the crash of capitalism and believed in socialism, civil rights, labor unions, and antifascism. While most communists supported the Soviet Union, which appeared to represent an enlightened economic system, they were still patriotic Americans. She was long haunted by her party affiliations, as were many others, but she would never abandon her political beliefs and commitments, despite the burdens and hardships. While the party took no official position regarding music, folk or otherwise, by the mid-1930s a leftwing folk music culture had arisen. This became particularly noticeable following World War II, when Pete Seeger, Woody Guthrie, and a host of others organized People's Songs to encourage and distribute topical songs. While People's Songs was not officially affiliated with the Communist Party, now struggling to maintain its membership and influence, there were nonetheless strong connections, of which Jenny was one.[1]

Jenny was also unique in that she lived in northern New Mexico, while most of her political and musical colleagues were in New York City, Los Angeles, Chicago, and other metropolitan centers. Yet she was never isolated from the national folk world. For example, she was a member of People's Songs' board of directors, and performed at their 1947 convention in Chicago, where she joined a "Coast-to-Coast Hootenanny" with Woody Guthrie, Pete Seeger, Earl Robinson, and others. Moreover, in San Cristobal she was surrounded by Hispanic folksongs, which she introduced to the larger leftwing folk world. She appeared with Seeger at the California Labor School also in 1947.

Her interests came together with the Henry Wallace Progressive Party presidential campaign in 1948. She performed at various party rallies as well as the party's convention in Philadelphia. She wrote at least one song for the campaign, "Skip to the Polls," based on the traditional "Skip to My Lou:" "Now Wallace is my partner, And Taylor too/Now Wallace is my partner, And Taylor too/And Wallace is my partner, And Taylor too/Skip to my Lou, my darling." (It must be noted that Jenny Vincent herself denies writing this song.) She apparently made no recordings at the time, however.[2] Following Wallace's defeat, and the escalating cold war, the political landscape began to shift to the right, with serious consequences for Jenny and many others. While she was geographically remote from the centers of political controversy, she yet could not escape from the pressures of the time. Harvey Matusow, for one, would bring the mounting Red Scare to her doorstep. Having grown up in New York City, and served during the Second World War, he had first joined the Communist Party and worked at the People's Songs office. But in early 1950 he decided to cooperate with the Federal Bureau of Investigation (FBI). On a trip to the West Coast during the summer, he stopped at the San Cristobal Valley Ranch and immediately began to identify for the FBI who was at the ranch, including labor organizer Clinton Jencks. He also supplied photographs. Matusow had heard about the ranch when Jenny performed in New York the previous year. For the next few years he served as a key anticommunist witness, causing much trouble for Jencks and his ranch hosts. While Matusow proved a thorn in their side, on a more pleasant note Earl Robinson served as their music director for a few years. "In the early blacklist years, I spent summers, 1949, 1950, and parts of '51 and '52, at the San Cristobal Valley Ranch," he would write. "Jenny, who married [Craig Vincent] after the war, fought the good fight her own way. A musician through and through, Jenny plays piano and also accompanies her lovely singing voice with a small accordion. I refer to her still as the 'Rocky Mountain Thrush.'" Robinson also recalled that the "ranch was an ideal place to research Mexican-American and Indian folklore." He was the noted composer of "Joe Hill," "Ballad for Americans," "The Lonesome Train," and numerous other staples of the left. An early casualty of the Red Scare, he was an invaluable addition to the ranch's staff.[3]

Through the 1950s Jenny kept up her musical and labor/leftwing life, although the ranch was soon abandoned, a casualty of political repression and economic hard times. Folk music also suffered for a few years, highlighted by the blacklisting of the popular Weavers, including Pete Seeger, by 1953. While folk music continued to carry a radical tinge, there was a growing popular audience by mid-decade, led by Harry Belafonte and the Tarriers. The latter originally included Alan Arkin, Earl Robinson's nephew, who had spent two summers at the ranch. While Jenny was never a vital part of the developing folk music revival, in 1952 she began a longstanding relationship with Sarah Gertrude Knott and the National Folk Festival, which began in St. Louis in 1934. While Knott was not known for any leftwing leanings, she preferred an eclectic lineup and had no problem enlisting Jenny as a performer. There were ethnic folk festivals scattered around the country in the 1930s, but as Knott explained, "Why not a National Folk Festival, bringing together groups from different sections of the country with their folk music, dances, and plays, to see what the story would tell of our people and our country." She initially included important folklorists, beginning with Vance Randolph, George Pullen Jackson, Bascom Lamar Lunsford, even Zora Neale Hurston. The festival mostly traveled from city to city, but by the 1950s it had lost much of its early luster and support. There was also competition from the emergence of the Newport and other popular folk festivals by the early 1960s.

Jenny's lack of recordings, except on her own Cantemos Records label, meant that her audiences were essentially limited to festival goers and those in and around New Mexico. For example, she also participated in the Fox Hollow and Idyllwild festivals, both with limited audiences. The former was organized by the singing Beers family in Petersburg, New York, in 1966 (it folded in 1980), and attracted a small but loyal following. The latter, while not exactly a festival, was formally known as the Idyllwild Arts Foundation School of Music and the Arts, and was located near Palm Springs in Southern California. Begun in 1950, it was an adjunct of the University of Southern California School of Music. Various musicians came and went each summer, with the versatile Sam Hinton a yearly presence, along with Bess Lomax Hawes, the sister of Alan Lomax. This was a chance for Jenny to combine her teaching and performing skills.

Her musical life continued through the century and into the next, when she was still recording. This was an incredible testament to her musical dedications and amazing ability to perform a wide range of styles, while still specializing in her bilingual repertoire.[4]

Jenny Vincent's life captures some of the history of folk music in the United States in the twentieth century, but from a peculiar perspective. She was friends through the years with many of the major performers and songwriters of the second half of that century, including Pete Seeger and Malvina Reynolds. Her music touched upon various aspects of the developing folk revival, and in the process demonstrated not only the close connection between folk music and leftwing politics, but also the staying power of both. Her commitment also to preserving the rich legacy of Spanish-language songs in the Southwest would remain one of her singular accomplishments. Her life is both an inspiration and indication of what one dedicated musician and organizer can do.

NOTES

1. For background, consult Richard A. Reuss with JoAnne C. Reuss, *American Folk Music and Left-Wing Politics, 1927–1957* (Lanham, Md.: Scarecrow Press, 2000).

2. Reuss and Reuss, *American Folk Music*, 237. "Skip to the Polls," *Songs For Wallace*, 2nd ed. ([N.Y.]: People's Songs, Inc., 1948), 5.

3. Robert M. Lichtman and Ronald D. Cohen, *Deadly Farce: Harvey Matusow and the Informer System in the McCarthy Era* (Urbana: University of Illinois Press, 2004), 34–36, 175–76; Earl Robinson with Eric A. Gordon, *Ballad of an American: The Autobiography of Earl Robinson* (Lanham, Md.: Scarecrow Press, 1998), 225–27.

4. For a reference to her ongoing influence on regional music, see Dan Margolies, "The Sandia Hots: Spicing Up Old-Time Music with the Sounds of the Southwest," *Old-Time Herald* 10, 5 (June–July 2006), 25. For an overview of folk music, see Ronald D. Cohen, *Rainbow Quest: The Folk Music Revival and American Society, 1940–1970* (Amherst: University of Massachusetts Press, 2002), chs. 3–4 and *passim*; and Guadalupe San Miguel, *Tejano Proud: Tex-Mex Music in the Twentieth-Century* (College Station: Texas A&M University Press, 2002).

Preface

Jenny Is My Paul Robeson
John Nichols

I was raised on folk music and blues and cowboy tunes and campfire favorites and college football fighting melodies. My father played the guitar and sang to his family all through my childhood. He taught me "Little Joe the Wrangler" and "Frankie and Johnny" and countless other wonderful songs. He sang tunes in Russian and in French, and he sang old sentimental favorites. I loved his renditions of "The Bluetail Fly" and "Big Rock Candy Mountain" and "Willy the Weeper."

I started playing the guitar at age fifteen, in 1955 when rock 'n' roll was new and extraordinary. Then I purchased one of those books by Alan Lomax. And I segued into the blues and Woody Guthrie and Leadbelly and Josh White and the Weavers and Champion Jack Dupree.

I spent the summer of 1961 sitting at the feet of blind Reverend Gary Davis up in the Bronx trying to learn "You Got to Move" and "Twelve Gates to the City."

I also branched out into ranchera tunes and Tex-Mex and country and western—Hank Williams, Tammy Wynette, Bob Wills and the Texas Playboys. Later on I even played some flamenco riffs so my wife could practice her dancing.

Oh, I remember occasions in college and for years afterward when a bunch of us would gather on Saturdays and drink wine and smoke doobies and play music all night long. We never sang the same song twice. We knew so many tunes.

I loved that music for its sheer exhilaration. I loved it because everybody knew the words. I loved it because it made connections between classes and across cultures. I loved it because it told stories. There were ballads and *corridos* and spirituals that we sang for civil rights, and that we sang against the war. We also sang songs at weddings and at funerals and at birthday parties. The music made me happy, made me sad, made me angry. I could use the music to seduce girls, I could use it to put my kids to sleep. I could use the music to celebrate . . . and believe me, I always used it to celebrate.

That's what Jenny Vincent has done all her life through music: she has celebrated. And this book certainly celebrates Jenny's life.

I am sixty-six years old now and I don't play much music anymore except all alone at three AM when I put on a CD by Jerry Lee Lewis or my old pal Malcolm McCollum, and follow their riffing for the sheer fun of it. But Jenny Vincent is still going strong in her *nineties*, and *in public*. I mean, she's still out there singing a thousand melodies, and that busts me up, it really does. It makes me happy.

Jenny has been a candle burning brightly in the hurricane for more decades than I have been alive. Today we understand that she has been one of the seminal teachers of our time. Like Pete Seeger, she's a really down-to-earth and very important icon, keeping the spirit alive, keeping the culture—Spanish, Anglo, Native, African-American, South American, you name it—alive.

Jenny has preserved precious music for future generations. She has kept a bilingual tradition alive. She has promoted the music of children and of the elderly. She has been a faithful and tireless worker for the joyous outbursts of song that define the peoples on earth.

I'm amazed by her strength and by her persistence. I'm grateful to Audrey Davis and Rick Klein for becoming a part of her music during the past decade. What can I say about the three of them together in the Jenny Vincent Trio? They *rock*.

You can sit down with Jenny and start to hum a tune, any tune. And an hour later you will have gone through a great repertoire of songs from all kinds of places and times in history and cultures. Cowboys, Indians, Elizabethan ballads, Mexican revolutionaries, Appalachian coal miners: "La Cucaracha," "Barbry Allen," "La Llorona," "Sixteen Tons."

For Jenny, one of the grand highlights of her musical career was accompanying Paul Robeson. One of the super highlights of my musical career was playing "Cielito Lindo" and "De Colores" with Jenny at my doctor's daughter's wedding in Taos. You know *why* that was so special? Because Jenny is *my* Paul Robeson.

Jenny and her husband Craig [Vincent] are among the most important friends I've ever had because they went about life with verve, with humor, and with an impeccable social conscience. They stood up for the lonely and for the underdogs. They stood up for immigrants and for social justice. They stood up for principles that I believe are a lifeline to any positive future humankind might hope to have on Earth.

Craig and Jenny always believed that people can make a difference. They flat out inspired me. And they knew how to laugh and really enjoy themselves, also.

I don't think Craig could carry a tune from the back door to the outhouse, but Jenny sure could and she still can. When you see a vital person like Jenny teaching us the joy of music in her mid-nineties, you simply have to take your hat off when she strikes the first note on her accordion.

Then you listen *very* carefully. Because this is historic. This is our past and it is our future. This lady is a big breath of hope in a cynical age. Every tune carries within it the tapestry of our souls.

The music is magic.

I thank Jenny Vincent and Craig Smith for the celebration contained within this lovely book.

June 22, 2006

Acknowledgments

First and foremost: Jenny Vincent. This has been a labor of love for my wife and myself, and we and anyone who reads this book have Jenny to thank for it. For her generosity, her indomitable spirit, and her personal warmth, we remain in her debt.

My first writing mentor—and a friend ever since—was the poet Ronald H. Bayes. He set me on the path—though this first tangible result took somewhat longer than he might have imagined! Thanks also in so many ways to teacher, mentor, and dear friend Richard C. Prust. Here's to those many years of summer walkabouts in the city, Dr. Dick. And to another role model, my friend the historian Joel Williamson.

For their lasting friendship and continuous encouragement, love and thanks to Mary de Rachewiltz and Patrizia de Rachewiltz. And to one who, despite his untimely passing, remains an inspiration: Jeffrey Willer. *Kalo taxidi!*

At New York University I had the good fortune to study with three men who proved to be mentors, friends, and writing role models: Paul Baker, Carl Prince, and Kenneth Silverman. I also worked for twenty years with many wonderful people at NYU, among them Lynne P. Brown, John Beckman, and all my former colleagues in the Office of Public Affairs, particularly my writing buddies Barbara Jester and Jason Hollander, who listened beyond the call of duty.

Special notes of gratitude go to Valerie Sauers, to whom I owe so much, and to two irreplaceable friends, Janet and Barry Spanier.

My stepson, Jay Foley, introduced me to Jenny's music, which in turn inspired this project. So to Jay and all my New Mexico family—Donna Longo Foley, Alison Foley Dicks, and Merrill Dicks—thanks for your support and patience. My brother, D. Culver (Skip) Smith III, always encouraged me to go my own way, and I thank him for his counsel. Thanks as well to *mi amigo* Wally McCall, who never doubted that someday . . .

Viva archivists everywhere! Specifically, in this case, Eric Hillemann at Carleton College, the staff of the Sarah Gertrude Knott Archives at Western Kentucky University, and Gail Malmgreen at New York University's Tamiment Institute.

Many people have touched and been touched by the life of Jenny Vincent, and this book reflects the contributions of those who shared their recollections, stories, anecdotes, and feelings with me. I spoke with and benefited greatly from Helayne Abrams, Alan Arkin, Ellen Baker, Floy Barrett, Dorie Bunting, Kim Chernin, Judson Crews, Audrey Davis, Roxanne Dunbar-Ortiz, Betty Ferry, Frank Ferry Jr., Dee Fleming, Jock Fleming, Henry Foner, Linda Gordon, Phaedra Greenwood, Junella Haynes, Clinton Jencks, Rick Klein, Terry Klein, Jim Levy, Elizabeth "Betita" Martinez, Tommy Martinez, Peggy Nelson, Ruth Rael, Rena Rosequist, Mark Rudd, Mildred Tolbert, Jose Leon Trujillo, Valentina Valdez, Maria Varela, Enriqueta Vasquez, and Mary Wheeler.

John Nichols not only encouraged the project and spoke with me at length, but opened portions of his own files to me. Thanks to John also for his preface to the book, as well as to Ronald D. Cohen for his foreword.

Jenny's sons Larry, Michael, and Dimi supported the project without hesitation, spoke openly with me, and sometimes encouraged Jenny into greater detail.

I owe a great deal to Jenny's niece, Mary Deborah RioGrande. "Mary D" has not only given splendid organization to portions of Jenny's archive, she conducted primary research for this book and was endlessly supportive.

From the first time my wife and I sat down with Jenny, it became clear that no single interview could begin to capture the long, full life of Deborah Jeannette Hill Wells Vincent, a life that began before World War I and continues to hum with activity. This book is an attempt to do justice to that life, but there would have been no book at all without the guidance of David Holtby, former editor at the University of New Mexico Press. David and CounterCulture Series coeditor David Farber read the original manuscript and made invaluable suggestions that helped shape the book's final form. My sincerest thanks also to managing editor Maya Allen-Gallegos and all of her colleagues at the press who worked on this project.

The final word of thanks goes to my wife, Lynda, who contributed to every part of the book and the process that went into it. She was an integral part of the interviews with Jenny upon which the book is founded, read the manuscript at all stages and made excellent suggestions, and endured the writing and rewriting with patience beyond all reasonable limits. *Mil y mas.*

Introduction

Wild Horse Mesa is a stretch of ground along Highway 159 in southern Colorado that extends from the town of San Luis to the New Mexico state line. In daylight and at sixty or more miles per hour, you might pass through the mesa in fifteen minutes, barely aware of Blanca Peak in the Rocky Mountains behind you or the Sangre de Cristo Mountains on your left. On a starless night you can feel the pitch darkness tighten around you.

At 11:30 one night in the late spring of 2003, the headlights of a small van were the only stars that cut through the dark on that part of the road. Inside, amid assorted musical instruments and sound gear, the members of the Jenny Vincent Trio had fallen silent. It had been a successful evening for violinist Audrey Davis, guitarist Rick Klein, and accordionist and singer Jenny Vincent. The trio had played its signature blend of international folk songs, Mexican and New Mexican polkas and waltzes, and cowboy ballads to a full house at a restaurant in La Veta, a small town at the foot of Colorado's Spanish Peaks. The trio finished its three-hour set at 9:30, and an hour later had been paid, fed, and packed into the van. A two-hour drive lay ahead of them, yet they wanted to return to New Mexico the same night: they were to perform at the Fiesta de Taos the next day. Now they were quiet as Terry Klein, Rick's wife, drove toward Taos and home.

In the front passenger seat, Jenny was wide awake. That night she had recognized familiar faces in the audience, as she always does, but also old friends she had not seen in years, friends who reminisced with her after her performance. Jenny does not dwell in the past, but when she does reflect on it she can draw on nearly nine decades of memories. They begin with the sound of bells that announced the end of the First World War. In her time Jenny has been hailed for her work in public schools and harassed for her progressive politics. She has sung for war veterans and women on picket lines but never for FBI informants or McCarthyite committees. In all that time she has never wavered from her work with music as a means to break down barriers between people.

Suddenly, the headlights of the van illuminated a herd of wild horses crossing the highway ahead. Terry slowed the vehicle to let them pass, and Jenny watched the horses glance in her direction and continue across the road. As they slipped away into the night, they drew Jenny's thoughts back over the people and places of her long life.

ONE

Gifts of a Lifetime

By the time Jenny was four years old, she had made her performance debut with a brief recitation in church—

Birdy with a yellow bill
hopped upon the window sill,
cocked his eye and gamely said,
"Ain't you 'shamed, you sleepy head?"

She also had launched her lifelong love affair with the piano, and got her mouth washed out with soap at an early age for saying the word "fart." Two of her brothers thought it would be the perfect prank to teach their little sister a forbidden word. They did, and when she repeated it to her father, a minister, he responded with a spanking and a soap-laden toothbrush.

The soapy toothbrush incident is the only unpleasant memory among the few that Jenny has of her father, Fred Burnett Hill. Fred was born in 1876 to Edwin Frederick Hill and Grace Jeannette (Squire) Hill of Red Wing, Minnesota. He earned a bachelor of literature degree in 1900 from Carleton College in Northfield,

Minnesota, where he was a baseball player as well as a scholar, and a bachelor of divinity degree in 1903 from Hartford Theological Seminary. It was while he was serving as associate pastor of the Central Congregational Church in Providence, Rhode Island, that he met a young woman named Deborah Wilcox Sayles.

While Fred hailed from people who considered themselves Minnesota pioneers, Deborah was a descendant on both sides of permanent Rhode Islanders. Her father, Frederick Clark Sayles, traced his lineage to the state's founder, Roger Williams, and was proud of it. An honors graduate of Providence Conference Academy, Frederick started his career as a day laborer in his brother's bleachery. By the time he and Deborah Cook Wilcox married, in 1861, he was on his way to a partnership in the firm. Over the next three decades the Sayles brothers expanded into railroads, mills, and utilities, amassing a fortune estimated at $20 million. Frederick also served as Pawtucket's first mayor. He and his wife passed on their political conservatism, appreciation of the arts, and sense of community responsibility to their children, including Jenny's mother.

Deborah Sayles was born in 1880 and grew up the belle of Bryn Mawr, her family's sixty-five-acre estate. She could sit on the front steps of a red brick mansion that was filled with paintings and sculpture from Europe and look out over cultivated gardens, grounds, and greenhouses. She appeared to want for nothing. But in 1895 Deborah's mother died unexpectedly, and in 1902, on what would have been her mother's sixty-first birthday, the twenty-two-year old Deborah was still grieving. "My dear dead Mother out some where in the wide summer night, I write a note to you," she confided in her diary. "I am such a lonely girl! I have nobody to speak to. Mother, don't forget me in your grand heaven!" That same year her father suffered a stroke, rallying only long enough to dedicate the Pawtucket library in his late wife's name.

When Fred Hill entered her life Deborah was no stranger to suitors, several reputedly among European royalty, but the only one she took seriously was a Yale University student from Illinois named Frank Ferry. However, Frank could not dislodge Fred. The engagement drew storybook headlines from the society pages: "Beautiful

Heiress Spurns Rich Suitors; to Wed Poor Pastor." It was a love match, yet it also demonstrated Deborah's independence of mind and her determination not to become just another wealthy matron. "My future is not in society," she said. "I am tired of the ballrooms, the idle talk, the butterflies, the aimless lives. I want an opportunity to relieve suffering and support and encourage the work of uplifting humanity."

Fred and Deborah married in 1905 and embarked on an extended honeymoon to Europe and Asia, where Fred was as interested in visiting missions as he was in standard tourist sites. In 1906 they returned to Connecticut, where Fred began graduate work at Hartford Theological and Deborah gave birth to their first child, Mary. The following year they moved to Northfield, where Fred had accepted offers to teach at his alma mater and to serve as minister in a Congregational church.

Northfield straddles the Cannon River south of Minneapolis-St. Paul. The town's frontier days were behind it when Fred and Deborah arrived from the East, but its citizens still basked in the glory of having decimated the Jesse James gang during an attempted bank robbery the year Fred Hill was born. The Hills settled on College Avenue at the cusp of the Carleton campus, where daughter Mary was followed by Fred Jr. (Bud), born in 1908; Robert, in 1910; Edward (Ned), in 1911; and, on April 22, 1913, Deborah Jeannette. Jenny weighed eight-and-a-half pounds and was all good health. "Oh, Jenny," Mary told her years later, "I was so happy when Papa told me I had a baby sister."

When Jenny was born, Woodrow Wilson was barely fifty days in the White House, and south of the Mexican border Pancho Villa was ready to test the new president's mettle. At home and abroad suffragettes were on the march, while Henry Ford was busy adapting the conveyer belt for his auto works. "Scientific management" and "go-getter" were current phrases. In Paris, Stravinsky's *The Rite of Spring* caused a near riot, while New Yorkers were wowed—or appalled—by their first glimpse of European modern-ist painting. Vaudeville was still in vogue, and audiences laughed along with Sophie Tucker and Sir Harry Lauder, whose recordings Deborah Hill enjoyed.

After Jenny was born, Fred and Deborah donated their house to Carleton College and built a new home around the corner on Third Street, a three-story brick colonial mansion complete with gardens, tennis court, full basement, and garage with apartment. Deborah began to put her wealth to use through gifts to the college and charitable causes, while Fred, free of any need for personal gain, lent his own keen mind to numerous volunteer organizations. "He is easily the town's foremost citizen," a local newspaper said.

An accomplished pianist, Deborah resumed playing as soon as she was able after Jenny's birth. In time her new daughter began to crawl up beside her on the piano bench and try to imitate her. In addition to her mother's classical repertoire, Jenny heard popular songs from college students who boarded in the garage apartment, one of whom taught her her first folk song:

> I have a rooster, my rooster loves me.
> I put my rooster under the gooseberry tree.
> My rooster goes cable-cock-oo-oo-oo!
> As other men's roosters do my rooster does, too.

The family spent summers in New Hampshire or at the shore on Cape Cod. Everyone hiked, rode horses, and swam. In winter they skated on the frozen river and raced sleds down snowy slopes. For Jenny, it was a robust beginning.

Sarajevo, Bosnia, was a world away from Northfield's tran-quility, but there in June 1914 a Serbian nationalist shot and killed Archduke Franz Ferdinand, heir to the Austro-Hungarian throne, and his wife. By August failed diplomacy, smoldering national ambi-tions, and entangling alliances had drawn every major European power into the first global war. "World War I began like a summer festival—all billowing skirts and golden epaulets," wrote Dalton Trumbo, who would enter Jenny's life during the McCarthy period.

"Nine million corpses later, the wail of bagpipes would never again sound quite the same."

America remained neutral until 1917. Ultimately, 53,000 GIs would die in combat and 63,000 more from diseases and related causes. While Fred and Deborah Hill volunteered many hours on behalf of Liberty Loan, Red Cross, and other drives, the war became truly personal for them in the summer of 1918, when Fred left on an eight-week commission from the YMCA to visit soldiers in England and France. Upon his return, he embarked on an exhausting schedule of public appearances to describe what he had seen and to appeal for continued relief efforts.

At five o'clock in the morning on November 11, 1918, in a dining car in the forest of Compiegne, France, Germany signed a treaty to end the catastrophic conflict. In Northfield Jenny awakened in the night to the peal of church bells. Too young to fully comprehend their significance, she only understood that news had reached her hometown that touched off a celebration. Soon every fire department bell joined in the glorious cacophony. All across America people were waking up to headlines like the page-one banner of *The New York Times*: ARMISTICE SIGNED, END OF THE WAR!

Like everyone else the Hill family rejoiced on Armistice Day, but inside their home this exuberance quickly faded. Already weakened by his trip abroad, Fred's self-imposed regimen of as many as three speeches a day depleted his health. In January 1919 he contracted influenza during the postwar pandemic that would sweep the world claiming more than twice the casualties of the war, including 550,000 in America alone. Fred's case quickly progressed into double pneumonia and peritonitis. Even a last-minute blood transfusion failed to revive him. Family lore has it that among his last words to his wife were, "I hope you'll look up Frank." On January 29, not three months after the armistice, Fred Hill died. He was forty-two.

The same week Deborah lost nine pounds and began to feel nauseous. Two months later, she suffered the miscarriage of a son. To this day Jenny considers her father's death the first turning point in her life and her first direct encounter with life's uncertainty. And to this day the peal of bells can send her mind back to the memory of an international celebration of peace, a time of joy that became tragically merged with a personal and premature loss.

In the fall Deborah, at age thirty-nine a widow with five young children, visited her brothers in New England. On her return she stopped in Lake Forest, Illinois, for a reunion with Frank Ferry and Frank's mother, Abby. Abby Farwell Ferry had made it clear long ago that she would welcome Deborah as her daughter-in-law. Frank soon asked Deborah the question he had wanted to ask fourteen years earlier, and now he received the answer for which he had so patiently waited.

This time there were no headlines about an heiress marrying beneath her station. Frank was the grandson of John V. Farwell, a wealthy merchant whose eponymous company was the oldest dry goods firm in Chicago. During his career Farwell would count Marshall Field, Potter Palmer, and S. N. Kellogg among his partners. He also operated the XIT Ranch in the Texas panhandle, at three million acres the largest in the world at the time. Frank Ferry excelled at Lake Forest Academy and Yale University, where he was known for his intellect, compassion, sense of justice, love of humor, and powerful memory. After college, Frank entered his grandfather's firm. No one could accuse Farwell of doling out patronage for his grandson. Brilliant in mathematics, Frank was a financial whiz.

Deborah and Frank married in July 1920 and settled on Sheridan Road in Winnetka, a wealthy suburb of Chicago. Their house overlooking Lake Michigan was an Elizabethan mansion of more than twenty rooms, not including the seven bathrooms, staff quarters, and incidental storage and attic spaces. It sat on two-and-a-half acres and cost $100,000. There Frank could indulge his passions for gardening and birds, interests he would pass on to his youngest stepdaughter.

Jenny adored her stepfather and new grandmother. She had never known her maternal grandparents, and Edwin Hill, her only biological grandparent living at the time of her birth, had died in 1919. Abby's devotion to the Hill children was critical to their adjustment into a new life, yet Frank was the key. To Jenny he became the paragon of fatherhood: "He accepted us five brats with open arms." Soon enough all the Hill children grew to love their stepfather. By the time Bud, Bob, and Ned were teenagers they had dubbed him "Duke." This was not because Frank Ferry was imperious. The nickname just seemed tailor-made for a man who was so successful yet who carried himself with such understatement.

While Frank worked hard at the family business and Deborah equally hard managing the family, the combined Ferry-Sayles wealth allowed them to employ a full domestic staff. They converted this freedom from many routine tasks into time spent with the children. Frank and Deborah were politically conservative—one did not find leftist publications in their house, or socialist politics in their dinnertime conversation—yet liberal with their children. With only seven years separating the Hill children, Jenny was never a distant youngest child trying to catch up. She enjoyed active, competitive sports. Attracted early to language, among her favorite pastimes were the word games Abby led at the dinner table. From banister sliding to touch football, card games to categories—a homemade precursor to today's "Jeopardy"—the Ferry house hummed with activity. And soon Jenny had a half-brother, Frank Jr., born in 1922.

Later in her life Jenny would describe her childhood as privileged. Her formative years were spent in the embrace of a family that was wealthy, cultivated, and stable, a background that in the future would make her highly sensitive to what many other people lacked. She had arrived in Winnetka at the outset of the Roaring Twenties, a decade of transformation in America, but little seemed to disrupt Jenny's life on Sheridan Road or at Black Oak Lake, Wisconsin, where the Ferrys had a rustic compound. She was too young to be aware of labor strikes sweeping the nation or of the heavy-handed crackdowns on them by authorities who feared a Bolshevik-like workers revolution. Labor strife and red scares would enter her life soon enough. At the moment, she was on the brink of a musical breakthrough.

Having started piano lessons in Northfield, Jenny now resumed them in her new home. Her teacher was Kathleen Air, who taught at Chicago's Columbia School of Music and maintained a small studio in Winnetka. While Jenny had studied notes during her previous lessons, Kathleen freed her with the musical gift of a lifetime—the ability to play by ear. She taught her new pupil chords and chord progressions using a number system that Jenny could apply to transpose songs into all keys. Kathleen also taught Jenny ragtime's syncopated left hand, made her familiar with the entire length of the keyboard, and had her play along with recordings of different musical styles. These were the most important four years of piano training in her life. In the third grade Jenny was memorizing complete songs, and by the time she was in seventh grade she could play anything she heard. "Not a day goes by," Jenny says, "that I don't bless Kathleen Air."

Jenny and her mother adored such popular singers as Kate Smith, Nelson Eddy, and Jeannette McDonald. Among Deborah's particular favorites were Paul Robeson's recordings of spirituals. She snatched up every 78 he released until he became too political. (To Jenny, Robeson remains a hero.) Mother and daughter likewise shared a love of musical comedy, heard Rachmaninoff play, attended concerts by John Philip Sousa, and saw Pavlova dance "Swan Lake." For Jenny, music was everywhere.

In 1926, as Jenny approached seventh grade, her parents enrolled her in North Shore Country Day School, a recently founded private school in Winnetka. Jenny's sister Mary had done well in a small school environment (her mother's alma mater, the Lincoln School in Providence, Rhode Island), and the family was convinced that a similar experience, particularly one so close to home, would be the right match for Jenny. Perhaps no other decision affecting Jenny's educational development had a more lasting, positive impact on her life.

The school's cofounder and headmaster, Perry Dunlap Smith, was a protégé of progressive education pioneer Francis W. Parker. He wanted North Shore to offer a curriculum that did not segment student minds into conventional channels but opened them to new ideas. Smith also advocated community. All students were to be invited to school proms; all students should participate in annual musical productions. Everyone, in other words, should have the opportunity to make good in all areas of education, from art and academics to sports and shop. The scholastic and social lessons of North Shore Country Day School would have a profound effect on Jenny. She thrived in the school's environment and enjoyed its proximity to home (she once went to school and back on a pogo stick). North Shore's four-point code of community, democracy, artistic and physical development, and global consciousness would shape her views on education and community.

At North Shore Jenny received her formal introduction to folk music, learning English versions of songs from around the world. This would encourage her lifelong performing style—playing and singing international songs in their original languages as well as in English. One of her texts was *The Home & Community Song-Book* compiled by Archibald Davidson and Thomas Surette. Jenny remembers Surette performing for a North Shore assembly and demonstrating on the piano how classical music often draws on folk themes. It was further evidence to her of the vital importance of folk music, a lesson she never forgot. She also put her own piano skills to work in a school swing band that performed such standards of the day as "Tiger Rag." Her prowess on the piano led Deborah Ferry to entertain thoughts of a concert career for her daughter, but Jenny herself had no specific plans in that regard beyond the certainty that music would always be at the center of her life.

During the summers of her high school years, Jenny attended Camp Arden, a girls' camp in Vermont that offered drama, dance, and chorus in addition to outdoor activities. Arden's director was Shakespearean actress Katherine Everts. "Everything in the camp was named for Shakespeare," Jenny recalls, "even the bathrooms!" It was at Arden that she performed in "The Children's Crusade," a play written by a fellow camper's mother, Elizabeth Morris. The play's closing line would later inspire Jenny to voluntarily perform in public schools: "The children of the world shall save the world." While music was the hub of Jenny's life, it did not receive her exclusive attention. She served in student government and was an avid athlete. Her favorite sports were field hockey and basketball, and she shared with her stepfather a love of pool. She was also playing a lot of tennis with a school football star.

Tall, blond, and handsome, Harry K. "Dan" Wells was an academic as well as athletic standout. He was in eighth grade, Jenny in seventh, and Fran Wells, Dan's sister, in sixth when the three met. In no time they formed an inseparable triumvirate. While Fran became Jenny's best friend, Jenny and Dan became engaged. "Maybe that is what made my mother's hair turn gray," Jenny says. "She must have wondered about this daughter of hers." Jenny's brothers immediately rose to the occasion. "Here comes Jeannette," they chanted. "Body by Fischer, legs by Steinway, necks by the hour."

Dan had every intention of attending Harvard. Jenny's family naturally expected that she would attend Carleton, after her father, sister, and brother Bud. In the summer of 1929, Jenny and Dan sat down for a serious heart-to-heart. If you go to Carleton it will mean the end of us, he told her. It's coeducational and a long way from Harvard. Their talk turned to Vassar College. Located in Poughkeepsie, New York, Vassar was only 200 miles from Harvard, a distance that paled in comparison with the 1,400 miles between Cambridge and Northfield. There was also a family legacy: both Dan's mother and Abby Farwell Ferry were Vassar graduates. When Jenny mustered up the courage to break the news to her parents, Deborah Ferry swallowed her disappointment but Frank Ferry was quietly pleased.

In the fall Jenny entered her senior year with Dan Wells on her mind and Vassar College on her horizon. She was vivacious, naturally curious ("Now Jean-ette," as one teacher always called her, "your problem is you always want to know why; the important thing is to know how"), and excited about her future. Having known every financial advantage, Jenny had also received from her family gifts that transcend affluence—love, intelligence, and physical health. At age sixteen, she stood five-foot-four with blond hair and luminous blue eyes. Jenny was outwardly oriented. She was not a loner but a joiner who thrived in her two small communities of family and school. At the end of the school year her class yearbook would single out her sunny disposition, adding, "Her music hath charms to please the ear; her beauty hath charms to thrill the eye."

Jenny was only one month into her senior year when America's Roaring Twenties party came to an abrupt end. On October 29, 1929, the nation's financial markets plummeted in the single most catastrophic day in their history. While the Ferry family businesses would endure, others began to fail. Jobs disappeared and life savings vanished. In a December message to Congress, President Herbert Hoover expressed confidence in the nation's economy. "What the country needs is a good big laugh," the president quipped. "There seems to be a condition of hysteria. If someone could get off a good joke every ten days I think our troubles would be over."

The Lawrence Trek

O n her first day at Vassar, Jenny heard the strains of a lone violin wafting down the hall in her dormitory as a fellow freshman played "Home Sweet Home." No one more adored her family than Jenny, yet for her there would be no separation anxiety upon entering college. It would prove to be the next phase in an already unbroken line of fulfillment in her young life. Founded in 1881, Vassar was in the business of producing young women who could think for themselves. Fresh from a solid academic experience at North Shore and not prey to romantic temptations, Jenny was ready to take full advantage of what Vassar had to offer.

She would major in piano and composition and minor in German, the latter due to the wealth of music materials written in that language—and a logical progression after her five years of Latin and French at North Shore. At Vassar she began to formalize all that Kathleen Air had taught her to do by ear. Intuition was now joined to theory, composition, and harmony, and her knowledge and skills grew quickly. To her studies she added, as she had at North Shore, generous helpings of extracurricular musical activity. She played the piano constantly. For three years she was the arranger and accompanist for a college vocal group called the Sextet ("All sweaters, saddle shoes, and bobby sox"). With classmate Francesca Eschweiler she composed the music for her class song, "Reaching Our Stride," with lyrics by another classmate, the future poet Muriel Rukeyser: "Before our faces Vassar's sign / Before us years we will define." Though tempered by time and hard reality, Jenny has never entirely abandoned that youthful idealism.

Unlike Rukeyser, who had already embraced liberal politics, Jenny would remain politically unformed during her college years. As the Depression deepened, many Americans were turning their eyes to the Democratic candidate for the presidency, a man who lived just up the road from Vassar in Hyde Park. Soon Franklin Delano Roosevelt would assume enormous importance to Jenny. Right now, however, she was preoccupied with the unanticipated troubles of the most important man in her life.

At Harvard, the unthinkable had happened. Dan Wells had arrived in Cambridge in the fall of 1929 fully expecting to excel. What he encountered was an institution too big and complex to easily conquer. Suddenly, the North Shore standout was just one of many who had been big men on their high school campuses. In a moment of lapsed judgment, he copied portions of a published article into one of his papers. It was only through the personal intervention of his father that Dan was not expelled for plagiarism. He received instead a one-year suspension. Humiliated, his family never spoke of the incident again. Some mutual friends expressed surprise that Jenny remained with Dan, but loyalty runs deep in her character—and she was in love.

Dan dropped out to work in an Illinois mining town. Here he came face-to-face with the grim working conditions, labor unrest, and poverty that would plague many Americans during the Depression, life-and-death struggles that put his Ivy League problems in stark perspective. It was also here that Dan first encountered the writings of D. H. Lawrence. The author was already a contentious figure when, in 1928, he published *Lady Chatterley's Lover*. Privately printed in Italy, the book became the most controversial novel in English of its time. Due to its explicit language and sexual content, it would remain officially unpublished in England and the United States for three decades, but pirated editions like the one Dan read in 1930—coincidentally the very spring Lawrence died—enjoyed wide if under-the-table circulation.

When he returned to Harvard in the fall, starting over at the same time Jenny entered Vassar, Dan began to make a name for himself. Football remained important, but his experience with miners as well as his exposure to Lawrence had planted seeds in his mind that would shape his life beyond sports. A philosophy major, his mentor was the towering thinker Alfred North Whitehead. Dan heard the philosopher praise the Romantic poets Wordsworth, Coleridge, and Shelley for their opposition to scientific materialism, an eighteenth-century mentality that accepted scientific ideas at face value.

Dan began to formulate a theory that Whitehead and Lawrence had reached similar conclusions in their thinking, the professor through the pure reason of philosophy and mathematics and the writer through literature and direct experience. As Dan saw it, the challenge posed by Whitehead and Lawrence was nothing less than the rescue of mankind from its descent into materialism and mechanization. As the nation entered the Depression, many Americans feared their country's era of economic growth was finished and that the times signaled the death knell of capitalism—a compelling argument that humanity could not be saved by technology alone. In this atmosphere, the ideas of Whitehead and Lawrence held great attraction for Dan.

While Dan contemplated Lawrence and Whitehead, Jenny remained centered on music and sports. "That was always a struggle for me," she says. "If I had given up sports I probably would have been a better pianist and done more in music. But I just had to play field hockey and basketball. I loved them!"

For piano instruction Jenny had the splendid fortune to follow Kathleen Air with Marta Milinowski, a former student of world-famous pianist Teresa Carreno of Venezuela. Jenny was to meet another brilliant South American pianist while at Vassar, Guiomar Novaes of Brazil. Arriving one afternoon before an evening concert, Novaes wanted to test out the piano she was to play that night. As a member of the college concert committee, Jenny escorted her to the auditorium where she would perform. It was winter, and Novaes's coat was missing a button. Jenny volunteered to sew it back on, so she sat down with needle and thread to sew—and listen—while the great Novaes practiced.

Studying with Milinowski and meeting with Novaes are musical milestones in Jenny's life, as is a New York City concert she attended by the celebrated Ignace Paderewski. Her Vassar years were swift and bright, bracketed by "Reaching Our Stride" and her "Baccalaureate Hymn," which she composed for lyrics adapted from Sir Thomas Browne and Sir Francis Bacon by Margaret Miller and future poet Elizabeth Bishop. During her undergraduate career Jenny achieved an enviable balance of team activities and individual pursuits, and she did not suffer the ambivalence that some students feel regarding their college experience. For Jenny, Vassar had been at the center of her world.

Jenny and Dan were married on June 20, 1934, eight days after her graduation. In ninety-nine-degree heat and humidity, Jenny wore her mother's wedding dress, veil, petticoat, stockings, slippers, gloves, and pearl necklace. "She looked like a queen," Deborah wrote. "They left in a motor boat, and we could see Jenny's little blue gloved hand wave for a long time."

The newlyweds set up housekeeping in Cambridge, but Dan was only one semester into his Ph.D. program when he decided he wanted to spend a term in Heidelberg, Germany, to attend lectures by philosopher Karl Jaspers. So in February 1935 Dan and Jenny booked a third-class cabin on the ship *Bremen* and were seen off in New York by Deborah Ferry and a group of college friends.

In Munich they purchased bicycles and a stack of Lawrence books, some of them in German. For Jenny and Dan, this was no quest for lost-generation thrills, no odyssey in search of the meaning of life. This was a pilgrimage they dubbed "the Lawrence trek." They launched a series of bicycle tours throughout the Bavarian countryside to sites where Lawrence and Frieda von Richthofen Weekley, newly lovers but not yet married, had traveled in 1912. As Deborah Ferry noted in her diary, "They feel they have found something very valuable in the philosophy of D. H. Lawrence and they need to digest it thoroughly before mingling with the herd." "They" was first and foremost Dan, yet soon enough Jenny was sharing his obsession. With their language facility and youthful ingenuousness they had little trouble meeting friends and relatives of Frieda.

In 1919 the Treaty of Versailles had forced Germany to cede the Saar Basin coalfields to France as compensation for its destruction of French mines and part of its total war reparations. Now, as the inhabitants of the Saar faced a treaty-mandated plebiscite to determine which flag the region would fly, Germany unleashed a massive propaganda campaign. Reeling from a series of internal economic and political crises and fearing its resurging neighbor, France told the League of Nations that it would not oppose the return of the Saar.

On March 1, 1935, Germany erupted in a celebration unlike anything in Jenny's experience. "It was one of the most colorful things I have ever seen," she wrote. "There were bands, parades of regiments—Nazis, policemen, and all." Germany, she noted, seems to be a united nation. In mid-March, Jenny and Dan headed south from Munich on their bicycles, the panorama set off by snowy mountain peaks against a sunny sky. The former college athletes had no trouble riding all day to Rottach-am-Tegernsee and an inn where the Lawrences had stayed. That same day, March 16, Hitler defied the Versailles treaty by reviving military conscription.

It was time for Heidelberg, the ancient university town that Fred and Deborah Hill had admired on their honeymoon thirty years earlier. Jenny and Dan immediately rode their bicycles across the Neckar River to Bachstrasse, where they were welcomed by Else von Richthofen Jaffe, Frieda Lawrence's sister. "We had a two-hour visit," Jenny noted. "Dan's eyes sparkled the whole time."

While the past was everywhere evident in the old town, the present could not be avoided. "Today we saw several groups of boys, in formation, marching and singing," Jenny wrote. "Before they disband they stand at attention and Heil Hitler!" Despite such ominous political signs, Jenny remained personally upbeat: "I can see that [Dan and I] are beginning a new, richer life together." Dan, however, seemed married first and foremost to his work on Lawrence. "I feel just like Frieda did," Jenny confided in her diary, "living with someone who is creating. Perhaps it is trying at moments, but the rewards more than make up for the trials." D.H.L., she noted, is our life.

Jenny balanced Lawrence with music. She memorized the entirety of Gershwin's "Rhapsody in Blue" and sang (in German) with a vocal group, the Madrigal Chorus. For her birthday, Dan surprised her with a small, 12-bass Hohner piano accordion. Jenny had never touched an accordion, but with her facility on the piano and her ability to both sight-read music and play by ear, she made rapid progress. Accordions would become her signature instrument for the rest of her life.

Dan was now attending Jaspers's lectures. For Jaspers, who coined the term "Existenzphilosophie" as a reaction against conventional thinking, any effort to understand existence required careful self-analysis and a personal quest for authenticity. Dan saw this position as a corollary to Whitehead's concept of philosophy as process and Lawrence's thirst for firsthand experience.

At the same time the university was becoming a frequent site for anti-intellectual rallies. "We are beginning to be very fed up with this Reich," Jenny wrote. "We hear nothing but Deutsches Reich, Deutsches this and that." One night, after witnessing yet another Nazi demonstration, Jenny and Dan turned for home singing "America" and "The Star-Spangled Banner." It was a brash and imprudent display, particularly in light of the warning Else Jaffe had given them: "Never talk politics in public!" They did not confess their behavior on a subsequent visit to the Jaffes, during which Else said she would mention them in a letter to her sister, who now lived in America.

In May Jenny and Dan attended a student meeting during which a professor declared that the duty of students is to rid the university of Jews and Jesuits. Nazism should be the one and only religion of the German people. While Dan and Jenny had not yet suffered any direct harassment, they were increasingly conspicuous. "Any time there were assemblies at the college they were all 'Heil Hitler! Heil Hitler!'" Jenny wrote, "and if you were the only ones who didn't stand and salute.... We were beginning to feel the pressure." With the approach of summer, they left Germany for England.

In London they bought Lawrence editions at Bumpus Books in Oxford Street and ate in restaurants where Lawrence had dined. Next they traveled to Eastwood, Lawrence's birthplace, where they met Jessie Chambers, perhaps Lawrence's first lover; Louisa "Louie" Burrows, once Lawrence's fiancée; Ada Lawrence Clarke, D.H.L.'s sister; John Middleton Murry, who with his companion Katherine Mansfield had been close friends of the Lawrences; Willie Hopkin, Lawrence's early mentor; and Hopkin's daughter, Enid Hilton.

Everyone in the Lawrence circle fell into one of two camps; the dividing line was Frieda. Hopkin and Hilton spoke highly of her but Burrows, Clarke, and Chambers had nothing good to say. Burrows read Jenny and Dan the letter Lawrence wrote her to break their engagement. Ada Clarke was bitter about Frieda and her brother. She showed Jenny and Dan one of Lawrence's notebooks in which her brother had written poems to his mother at the time of her death. Frieda had jotted in the margins "I hate it!" and "Good God!" To Jenny this was evidence of Frieda's struggle to rid Lawrence of his mother complex. Jessie Chambers (Wood) thought Lawrence had been completely changed for the worse when he went off with Frieda. She told Jenny that Lawrence's chief fault was that he thought he had an important message to give—that he was a genius.

The final destination on the Lawrence trek was Zinner, a village near St. Ives in Cornwall, where Jenny and Dan took a cottage. It was only fourteen feet square with a lean-to kitchen and his-and-hers outhouses, each with a view of the ocean, but it was the very cottage Lawrence and Frieda had rented in 1916. They were enchanted with Cornwall's jagged coastline and haunting, rock-strewn fields. "We are so excited," Jenny wrote. "Life changes for us from day to day. We don't even know what we'll be doing in another few weeks!" With only Dan's eventual return to Harvard to frame their plans, they could be flexible. Dan resumed his reading and Jenny her music on the accordion and a rented piano. They plowed through book after book ordered from Bumpus. At times the reading resembled an athletic competition. "Dan doesn't believe I'll even finish Moby Dick," she wrote, "but I'll show him."

Unlike the Lawrences, Jenny and Dan were not financially strapped: Jenny was now receiving an allowance from her grandfather's trust. Regardless, they threw themselves into the endless chores of rustic country living. The days were long and filled with tasks, but as photographs of Jenny's face from this time attest, these were invigorating days for her. She was increasingly drawn to a more simple life, and in this she was taking a lesson from the frugal example set by Lawrence and Frieda. Before leaving Heidelberg, Jenny and Dan had been invited by friends traveling through Germany to dinner at a posh hotel. They came home disgusted. "Imagine spending at least 100 marks a day!" Jenny jabbed into her diary. "Living in the best hotels, traveling always first class. Some people just don't know how to live!"

"Mussolini has mobilized," Jenny wrote on October 3, 1935. "The world is going mad." The next day newspapers reported that Italian planes were bombing towns in Abyssinia (present-day Ethiopia). Then, on November 27, a letter arrived. "Day of all days!" Jenny wrote. "Blue envelope postmarked N. Mex! A letter from Frieda Lawrence to Dan! How we did shout and shake. I met the postman when I went to get milk. When I saw that postmark with unfamiliar handwriting I jumped and nearly spilled all the milk and eggs, too. Dan read it aloud to me, and neither of us could speak or breathe." It was an invitation from Frieda to visit her in San Cristobal, New Mexico.

THREE

Mi Ranchito

"**S**weeping out of her colorful house dressed in a bright, Bavarian costume, eyes sparkling, and her smile greeting us very warmly," Jenny wrote in her diary, describing her first meeting with Frieda Lawrence. Jenny and Dan arrived in New Mexico in the summer of 1936 after a difficult spring. Just before they sailed from Europe in April, Dan had gone on a buying binge, purchasing Lawrence letters and other materials in Florence from Pino Orioli, who originally printed *Lady Chatterley's Lover,* and in London from Bertrand Russell. Jenny also spent hour after hour in the British Museum, copying Lawrence materials for Dan.

They returned to Boston with every intention of traveling on to New Mexico by car, but Dan appeared to be grappling with some emotional problems, about which he was uncommunicative, and he kept getting sick. Finally they traveled to Chicago and there boarded the California Limited for Lamy, the railroad station outside of Santa Fe.

"When we got up we found ourselves in the midst of mountains, sagebrush, and canyons," Jenny wrote. "It's like being in another world." The next morning they boarded a bus to Taos— getting out twice to walk, as many did who braved the bad roads in those days—and from there took another bus north to San Cristobal and Frieda's Kiowa Ranch.

The ranch had been a gift from Mabel Dodge Luhan. Daughter of a rich Buffalo banker, Mabel had arrived in Taos in 1917 after several marriages and liaisons, looking for a change from New York City, where she was the hostess of a celebrated Greenwich Village salon for artists, writers, political radicals, and Bohemians. Mabel had read Lawrence's *Sea and Sardinia*. Impressed with his depiction of Sicilian life, she invited him to Taos, hoping he would create a similar verbal monument to the local Tiwa Indians.

The Lawrences did come to Taos on three separate occasions between 1922 and 1925, and during one visit Mabel gave them the ranch and its 160 acres. Uncomfortable with possessions and wary about being beholden to others, Lawrence placed the ranch in Frieda's name. In exchange, Frieda presented Mabel with the original manuscript of *Sons and Lovers*, thereby canceling any indebtedness and undermining Mabel's penchant for manipulating those around her. Frieda promptly renamed the ranch for the Indian tribe that supposedly once camped on the mountain. When she came sweeping out of her door to meet Jenny and Dan, they were drawn irresistibly into her world.

During the ten days they spent in New Mexico that summer, Jenny and Dan met the leading figures of the Lawrence circle in Taos—writer Witter Bynner; Bynner's friend and one-time lover Willard "Spud" Johnson, founder of *Laughing Horse* magazine; and Lady Dorothy Brett, an English painter who had traveled to New Mexico with the Lawrences and stayed; as well as Mabel and her new Tiwa husband, Tony Luhan. They also renewed their acquaintance with Enid Hilton, who was now living there.

With his own agenda in mind—graduate school and a book on Lawrence—Dan thrust himself into negotiations between Frieda and Jacob Zeitlen, a Los Angeles bookseller to whom she had entrusted the sale of a collection of Lawrence papers. He hoped that Harvard would purchase the collection, where it would be immediately accessible to him. While Dan engaged Frieda in conversations involving his theory of Lawrence and Whitehead, Jenny and Frieda drew close on a personal level. Frieda's ebullient personality flowed over Jenny like a wave. She would join a roster of women role models for Jenny that included Kathleen Air, Marta Milinowski, and her own mother.

"I wasn't looking for the same things that Dan was, the deep thought, the intellectual side of everything," Jenny says. "I just remember Frieda as a true free spirit. She was so stimulating, and she was interested in bringing you out in conversation." They talked a lot about music. Enid Hilton told Jenny about the songfests that the Lawrences used to have, and how much Frieda enjoyed playing the piano and singing. That summer Jenny often played the piano for Frieda. "She also talked about relationships, and I learned a lot from her," Jenny says. "I didn't know a lot about relationships between men and women."

Jenny also learned more about the art of simple living. As perpetual travelers with unreliable incomes, the Lawrences had become masters of frugality. Now Frieda and Capt. Angelo Ravagli— "Angelino," whom she would finally marry in 1950—continued to live in that manner. Their example was an important factor in Jenny's ultimate decision to remain in San Cristobal.

Staying in New Mexico became a realistic possibility when Jenny and Dan went riding in the mountains one day with Diego Arellano, a young handyman at Kiowa Ranch. Arellano told them about an unoccupied ranch at the end of a high dirt trail. They climbed the steep, narrow path higher and higher through aspen groves. When they reached the ranch, Jenny and Dan let their horses into an abandoned corral and walked about admiring the view. Below them lay the beauty of Taos Valley and the Rio Grande Gorge. At their back stood pine forests and the skyline of the Sangre de Cristo Mountains. As she stood on the mountainside, Jenny suddenly felt that she had come home. At 8,000 feet, she was a mile and a third in the sky, but it was not altitude that affected her thoughts. Her response to the landscape matched Lawrence's of a decade earlier: "For greatness of beauty I have never experienced anything like New Mexico...the vast amphitheatre of lofty, indomitable desert, sweeping round to the ponderous Sangre de

Cristo mountains on the east, and coming flush at the pine-dotted foothills of the Rockies! What splendour!"

Back east that fall Dan arranged for the Lawrence collection in Zeitlin's safekeeping to be exhibited at Harvard and for Frieda to give a lecture there at the same time. Frieda and Angelino drove east ("Frieda couldn't believe they could cross state lines without having to stop and show their papers each time," Jenny recalls) and stayed with Jenny and Dan for two months. For the one formal affair they attended, Frieda contrived a memorable outfit. "She bought gold lame cloth from the Montgomery Ward catalog, cut a hole in the top and lined the neck and the sleeves with brown velvet," says Jenny. "It draped down over her like a poncho. She wore a brown velvet belt and a beautiful turquoise necklace. And tennis shoes!"

Frieda's lecture on Lawrence's poetry was a success, but when Harvard declined to purchase the Zeitlin collection for $25,000, Dan's preoccupation with D. H. Lawrence began to cool. He oversaw the return of the materials to Zeitlin with a curt cable, "the manuscripts are being sent to you today too bad." Frieda sensed that something else was cooling. "She may have suspected that Dan was doing all this with Lawrence just to make money," says Jenny, "although I don't think that was his motive. But aside from that, Frieda didn't like the way he was treating me, and she was probably right about that. I think he was living a separate life in his mind, and he had this compunction on the sexual side. Lawrence, of course, thought people should have many sexual partners, and Dan may have used that as an excuse. I didn't see it but Frieda did."

Nevertheless, in 1937 Jenny and Dan decided to buy the San Cristobal property. It was the depth of the Depression and real estate was inexpensive. The forty-acre ranch was theirs for $2,500. "We were twenty-four years old," says Jenny. "Our families thought we had flipped."

Jenny and Dan returned to New Mexico in the summer of 1937 to begin work on their property. In Cornwall they had hauled water, harvested crops, chopped wood, cooked under primitive conditions, mended their clothes, and built some incidental furniture. This, however, was a challenge of a different caliber. They were now the owners of a derelict property at the high end of a narrow valley overlooking a tiny hamlet occupied almost exclusively by Spanish-speaking people. Years later Jenny's neighbor Cleofes Vigil recalled what life in the valley was like at the time she arrived: "Old-timers like my grandfather were very much together, they weren't divided the way we are now. They believed in helping each other. And their trade was different from what it is now; they traded one product for another.... The old-timers, like my grandfather and father, they lived from their little farms, from their little land, land our ancestors left us."

While these country people may have been more self-sufficient than people struggling through the Depression in cities, men in the valley often had to supplement their farming by working for wages. They harvested potatoes, peaches, and apples in Colorado's San Luis Valley or herded sheep in Montana and Wyoming. It could be dangerous work. In 1939, Diego Arellano would go to Wyoming as a sheepherder. There he would contract Rocky Mountain spotted fever and die at the age of twenty-nine, leaving behind a wife and five children.

Jenny's ranch had a two-room cabin, several outbuildings, and a corral all in various stages of disrepair. There was no electricity, no telephone, no indoor plumbing, no paved road, and few automobiles. Yet the ruggedness of the place was part of its appeal to her. Like the farmers of Cornwall, the villagers of San Cristobal may have been skeptical of the newcomers at first, but they were friendly as well. "Our new neighbors taught us everything," Jenny says. "It was quite a turnaround for us."

In 1938 Jenny and Dan were back in Winnetka—Dan had put graduate school on indefinite hold and was teaching at North Shore Country Day School—when he and Jenny decided to start a summer camp at their ranch. During that first summer, staff and campers concentrated on restoring the ranch's physical plant. The following year Jenny and Dan looked for a project that would involve the whole community. There was a road from the bottom of the valley all the way up past the ranch, part of the old wagon road from Taos to

Questa, but it was in poor condition. They met with their neighbors to talk about rebuilding the road, and everyone agreed to pitch in. Men loaned their horses and wagons and worked on the project whenever they were home. When the job was completed, Jenny and Dan hosted a fiesta at their ranch, and more than two hundred people gathered to enjoy food, music, and dancing.

In the summer of 1940 Jenny and Dan again met with their neighbors, this time to sound them out about the possibility of establishing a new school in the valley for both local and boarding students. At the time children of San Cristobal attended a one-room village school with only one teacher—and that only through the eighth grade, after which they had to go to Taos. To the villagers, Taos was the city. They traveled there to stock up on provisions they could not provide for themselves, but didn't particularly like the idea of their children being away for long periods of time. Besides, a thirty-mile roundtrip over bad roads, especially in winter, was no cakewalk. So when Jenny and Dan proposed starting a school for grades nine through twelve, the villagers agreed. The road project had gone a long way toward creating a bond between the community and the ranch. The school clinched it. In 1940 Jenny and Dan decided to move permanently to New Mexico.

The decision was equal parts romance, rebellion, and response. As Jenny readily admits, she and Dan were romantics, "me more than him." The decision to buy a rundown ranch may have been impulsive, but Jenny was ready to establish her own life on her own turf. She was taking her mother's example to avoid an idle life to another level. Jenny was not interested in trying to establish a utopian or artisans' commune. She was determined that the ranch not be an isolated outpost but part of the surrounding community, and she worked hard to establish relationships with her new neighbors. In the end, Jenny was smitten with the people of San Cristobal. She responded to their warmth and humor, their can-do attitude, and their folk music traditions. "I had landed in a valley of people who were the salt of the earth," she says. "To me, it all came together in San Cristobal."

San Cristobal Valley School rose on stones gathered from the fields and tiles that came from the state penitentiary. The public school system supplied textbooks and a hot lunch program and before long asked Jenny and Dan to add grades five through eight.

Fran Wells joined the founding faculty of Jenny, Dan, Charles Marsh, and Ramon Cordova. Jenny taught music appreciation, harmony, piano, German, French, and Latin. Dan and Fran covered English, history, social studies, and art and art appreciation. Marsh, from the Todd School in Barrington, Illinois, taught science and mathematics while Cordova, a linguist from Dixon, just south of Taos, taught English to Spanish-speaking students and Spanish to English speakers.

The education at San Cristobal Valley School was modeled after North Shore Country Day School. "We tried to establish a curriculum that would meet the needs of both local children and boarding students," Jenny says. "A lot of it was built around the things kids did together—chores, building, caring for their own rooms, outdoor activities. Both groups learned something about the importance of working together and doing things as a community." Classes began at 9:00 AM. After a recess, Jenny would head for the kitchen to help with lunch preparation. Classes resumed at 1:30 PM, followed by a work period at 3:30 during which everyone pulled beans, picked apples, and performed whatever chores needed doing. No one had trouble falling asleep at night.

Jenny and Dan adopted a policy whereby boarding students paid tuition but local students did not. At that time the average annual cash income per family in Taos County was less than $200, and the infant mortality rate one of the highest in the nation. More often than not, however, the villagers paid in kind with sacks of potatoes or pinion nuts, even animals. Jenny and Dan also launched a series of community nights, when everyone could come to the ranch for games, art activities, music, and dancing.

In 1941 another event at the ranch attracted the attention of San Cristobal: Jenny was pregnant. Everyone seemed to have an opinion on what to name the baby. In September Frank and Deborah Ferry arrived to await the birth. Deborah was impressed at all that Jenny and Dan had accomplished—and all that still needed to be done. "Everything is at once complete and incomplete," she wrote. "I call it pioneering!" Pioneering it may have been, but Deborah marveled at how her daughter managed it all: "Jenny is certainly a wonder." What Aldous Huxley had said of D. H. Lawrence could now be said of Jenny—he regarded no task as too humble for him.

Several days before Jenny's due date the entire family checked into a hotel on the Taos Plaza to be closer to the hospital. Day after day went by, broken up only by meals, movies, and chatting with hotel guests from Hollywood who were in town filming "Valley of the Sun" for RKO. Jenny's water broke on a Saturday night while she was in a movie theater, but for two more days nothing happened. Deborah, recalling her own difficulties at Jenny's birth, was near hysteria. Finally, early on October 7, 1941, Jenny gave birth to a baby boy. "Jenny went to the hospital last Sunday morning with pains coming every two or three minutes," Deborah wrote Jenny's sister, Mary. "Poor child was about worn out when the final pains began, and early this morning about three o'clock the Dr. decided it would have to be either forceps or Caesarian—and he decided on forceps. It took three doctors to extract the baby. He weighs seven-and-one-half lbs. and is a lusty crier."

Jenny almost died. The birth had been a fifty-two-hour ordeal. The next day Deborah wrote to Mary, "Jenny is not feeling very comfortable because of the 6 stitches she had to have. . . . She had a very serious time. Dr. said the baby would never have arrived if he hadn't been so husky and well." One day later: "Dan described him as having a cauliflower ear, a black eye, and a head shaped like a pueblo. . . . Poor little baby did look pretty bad, but you never could believe he could improve so fast." The baby had strong lungs and a strong heart, and he was going to be all right. But Jenny's prognosis was guarded. She had a tumor in her uterus, contracted an infection, and had a temperature of 106. Deborah wrote Mary, "[Jenny] told me yesterday with almost tears in her eyes that she isn't getting along as well as she should." Heavy doses of sulfradiazine were causing her to have nightmares. She had to be fed intravenously. Her milk dried up, and she could not nurse the baby. She remained in the hospital for two weeks, under constant care from hospital nurses as well as Gretchen Skinner, the ranch nurse. Finally, Jenny awoke one day to find Gretchen collapsed across her bed, weeping. "Your temperature is normal," she said.

The long scare was over. Now they turned to another matter. The baby was two weeks old and still unnamed. "Well, you wouldn't be here if it wasn't for D. H. Lawrence," Deborah said, "and Frieda is to be his godmother." Lawrence it was—immediately shortened to Larry. Jenny and Larry went home. She was unable to resume teaching or much else around the ranch for some time, and she worried about Larry. Her doctors proved correct: Larry had a strong constitution and he soon achieved normal weight. Jenny was anxious for life to return to normal, but that would have to wait. Two months after Larry's birth, Japanese planes bombed Pearl Harbor.

In June 1942 Dan was back east, collecting the next batch of summer campers. When he returned in July, Dan also brought a new nurse for the ranch. Joan Hamilton was a friend of Gretchen's, who had gone back to Illinois. Jo is a real addition, Jenny wrote, and carries on like Florence Nightingale. The Wellses could use all the help they could get. The workload at the ranch only grew, while money was becoming tight. "Considering the state of the world in general," Jenny wrote her mother, "we have gone much too fast, as we well realize, and we can assure everyone that we have stopped expanding now. Our theory in the spending was to get things we needed while we could and building while we could still build."

One year to the day after Pearl Harbor, news reached San Cristobal that the federal government was acquiring the Los Alamos Ranch School and several thousand acres around it for unspecified military purposes—what would become the Manhattan

Project, the development of the atomic bomb. "We'd never want to sell, but perhaps there would be a chance of renting to the government for some kind of school or convalescent home for soldiers," Jenny wrote her mother. "We are listed among those places in New Mexico which have a large capacity." Jenny had no way of knowing how ironic her comment would prove in the future, when she and her ranch would appear on government lists of an entirely different sort. At the moment, she had more on her mind.

"Jo has departed for California to see her Bob and then to go into the army," Jenny wrote her mother in January 1943. "After she has seen Bob she'll go home to Maine to wait for her call. We're certainly going to miss her." Jenny could not bring herself to tell her parents what had really happened. "My husband began to show signs of excess interest," she says. "They started an affair right under our noses. I'm sure I didn't handle it well." Whatever words were exchanged, whatever agreements were or were not made, Jenny does not recall. She was humiliated—and outraged. So was Fran Wells, who thought her brother should leave immediately. Beyond the pain the affair caused Jenny, Fran was scandalized by its effect on the whole school. Dan decided to go to New York while awaiting induction into the army.

Dan Wells had always been a restless man, one who liked the initial excitement of a new project but quickly became bored with routine. Under the circumstances, the war offered him a means of escape. Jenny bitterly recalled how Frieda Lawrence had read the signs several years earlier. Within days of each other Dan and Joan left the ranch, he heading east and she supposedly to California. Several years would pass before Jenny learned that, shortly after their departures, a mutual acquaintance saw them coming out of a hotel together in Kansas City.

FOUR

Keep the Home Fires Burning

All across America men and women on the home front were meeting the extraordinary circumstances of war with inventiveness and ingenuity. Millions relocated to work in government offices, shipyards, and defense plants. Women became the backbone of these industries, the rise of which would help spell the end of the Depression. Millions more stayed at home and on farms, rationing gasoline and collecting rubber and other materials during wartime recycling drives. The rapid transformation of the country, particularly for American women, was stunning.

Jenny entered the war years as a single mother saddled with a ranch threatened by mounting debt. With her in the winter of 1942–1943 were Fran Wells and Sarah Tepping. Fran, who had lived so long in her brother's shadow, had come into her own at Vassar College, where she was a year behind Jenny, and matured into an effective teacher. She had recently married a man named Fred Gunther, who briefly taught at San Cristobal Valley School before enlisting in the Air Force. Sarah was a friend from Denver whose husband was

31

serving with the OSS in Italy. Alone together, the three women sat close to the fire on those cold New Mexico nights, sharing stories, reading letters from their husbands, and doting on Larry. Jenny, of course, listened with interest to such popular songs on the radio as "White Cliffs of Dover," "I'll Walk Alone," and "White Christmas," songs that spoke more of separation than had such World War I rallying cries as "Over There."

Jenny, Fran, and Sarah also nurtured each other with the reassurance of work, and there was much to be done. Jenny began to sell off whatever she could around the ranch, but still the debts piled up. "Our expansion has been too rapid for our income," she wrote her parents. "We shall be having to pay for a long time in the future for what we have built up." Frank Ferry responded with business advice and encouraging words. "We feel you and Fran are real pioneers alone on the ranch with so much to do."

In 1943 Jenny became Taos County educational director for the Rocky Mountain Farmers Union. The RMFU was founded in 1908 to help independent small farmers and ranchers in Colorado, New Mexico, and Wyoming improve and market their products. Legislation, cooperation, and education were its calling cards, and Jenny and Fran embraced the union's mission statement—stable farm and ranch families are the foundation of healthy rural communities, and healthy rural communities bolster the entire U.S. economy. Jenny's new duties included publicity, planning meetings, and visiting union groups throughout the county. She also helped establish local food and health cooperatives and publish *La Luz del Ranchero*, a small newspaper in Spanish for farmers. "I don't know how much you know about it or whether or not you approve of it," she wrote her parents, "but we are wholeheartedly for it and all it stands for. I feel that it's important to be part of such an organization in order to voice and act on one's beliefs in government."

The farmers union was a milestone in Jenny's personal and political maturation. In this work she found meaningful expression and practical applications for her growing political convictions. That same year she took a further step when she (and Fran) joined the Communist Party.

From its inception in 1919 the Communist Party USA had been the victim of suppression far out of proportion to its limited influence. It was also its own worst enemy, rent by internecine feuds and flip-flopping its names and policies. During the Depression, however, the apparent collapse of the capitalist economy made the party appear less sinister, not so much a stooge for the Soviet Union as a potential source of alternative economic and political solutions. American communists organized unions, campaigned for unemployment benefits, fought fascism during the Spanish Civil War, and promoted racial equality. It was one of many organizations that constituted the Old Left movement, and unlike some appeared to be actually doing something.

It was the party's finest hour, and it was short-lived. Its nagging allegiance to the Soviet Union was never more apparent than with the approach of World War II. When Hitler and Stalin signed a nonaggression pact in 1939, the party quickly assumed an antiwar stance. That position was just as abruptly reversed when Hitler subsequently invaded the Soviet Union. With the United States and the Soviet Union now fighting as allies, Jenny joined during the one window when the party was most publicly palatable and support for the Soviet Union even patriotic.

In the 1930s and 1940s the party attracted many intellectuals, artists, and musicians. Postwar repression would contribute to the decline of the party as a political force, but this cultural legacy would survive. While Jenny embraced the party's prolabor, antiracist policies, she was equally attracted by the left's widespread use of folk music and group singing. The music of the movement was as important to her as its politics, and she did not separate the two. She also had a personal reason for joining.

While teaching at North Shore Country Day School from 1938 to 1940, Dan Wells had joined the party, completing his own political odyssey begun in an Illinois mining town. Jenny felt insulted, not by the action itself but because Dan considered her a slow political learner and had not bothered to discuss his decision with her. Once before, on the Lawrence trek, Jenny had hurried to keep the pace with Dan. Now she took the extra step to avoid another gap between her and possible reconciliation with her estranged husband.

No political decision she ever made would have a more lasting or tumultuous effect on her life. At the same time, it would be disingenuous to belittle the sincerity of Jenny's political convictions. She was thirty now. She had lived in San Cristobal on-and-off for eight years, time enough to witness the struggles of people less fortunate than herself. In another letter to her parents she wrote, "It is so encouraging to find groups . . . that are concerned about racial discrimination, and are not only concerned but doing something about it. One has to belong to some organization to act forcefully."

In February 1944 Jenny attended a four-day RMFU workshop in Denver, learning how to plan programs that would teach young people an appreciation of farm life and rural culture and of their importance in developing it. On a lark, she had her fortune read in a downtown café. The fortuneteller told Jenny that she had artistic talent, especially in the art of singing. Your soprano voice is more than a bathroom warble, the clairvoyant said. You could go far if you choose to pursue a vocal career.

In fact, Jenny was already singing for RMFU events. That same month a Taos County public school teacher named Rufina Baca, who had heard about Jenny's performances for the farmers union, asked her if she would sing for her students. When Baca complained that local schools insisted they had no budgets for such frills as music, she was preaching to the converted. Jenny, the beneficiary of excellent music programs throughout her own schooling, considered music essential, not extracurricular.

As much as she herself loved music, Rufina Baca had a broader agenda that touched on one of the most contentious issues in New Mexico's public schools—the question of whether English or Spanish would prevail in the state's classrooms. In 1896 Amado Chaves, territorial superintendent of public education, wrote that it was a crime against nature and humanity to rob the children of New Mexico of the language that is their birthright and to deprive them of the advantages of being bilingual. The policy seesawed over the years until, by the time Rufina Baca approached Jenny, the use of Spanish in classrooms was officially prohibited. Jenny was appalled, particularly as more than 90 percent of the students in Taos County public schools were native Spanish speakers. She agreed completely with Baca, who was determined that her students not be denied their heritage, and accepted the teacher's invitation to sing to her students in Spanish on a voluntary basis.

Tommy Martinez was one of those students. Before his death in 2006, Martinez, a retired public school teacher, fondly recalled his former instructor. "Rufina Baca was my teacher in fourth grade in Questa, and she was very outspoken," he said. "At that time we followed the rule about not speaking Spanish in the classrooms or even during recess, but of course it didn't work. We could walk past the teachers' lounge and hear Spanish being spoken inside. Some administrator somewhere had decided that it would be better for our advancement if we spoke English all the time. Mrs. Baca said 'No!' And you didn't mess with her!"

It must have been an eye-opener for the Spanish-speaking students when Jenny arrived in their classrooms with a guitar and accordion to sing and teach them songs in their own language. With their short attention spans, children can be the toughest audience of all. They tend to be honest and they do not suffer fools. Jenny established an immediate rapport with them by never talking down to them and, perhaps most importantly, having them sing along with her. Baca had told Jenny that she was looking for an old song that contained in its refrain a sound like *'tin tin tin' (teen-teen-teen)*. Jenny found it in a book called *Spanish Songs of Old California*, compiled by Charles Lummis and Arthur Farwell. It was a traditional song called "Caputin," which is a raincape of leaves. When Jenny sang

> Do not kill me, do not kill me,
>   with a pistol or a knife.
> Kill me rather with your eyes, dear,
>   with your red lips take my life.
> With a caputin, tin, tin, tin, 'cause tonight it's going to rain,
> with a caputin, tin, tin, tin 'cause tonight it's going to rain

the eyes of the fifth and sixth graders went wide and the giggling was palpable. "That song is probably not one I would have chosen, but it certainly amused the kids!" Jenny defied the official policy by singing it in both languages.

At the same time she started singing for public school children, Jenny volunteered to entertain war veterans who were convalescing in Santa Fe's Bruns Hospital. There she once sang "Caputin" to a nineteen-year-old who was dying of tuberculosis. The young man opened his eyes and told Jenny she could not have chosen a better song—"My mother used to sing that to me." It was a defining moment for Jenny, one that confirmed once and for all her commitment to folk music as a powerful tool for direct communication. Folk music offered Jenny the kind of immediacy that she had not felt when playing the classical piano repertoire.

In June 1944, shortly after D-Day, Jenny returned to Bruns Hospital, playing the accordion and singing in ten different wards. One GI later told a Red Cross volunteer, "That girl did more for the morale of the men than any movie actress could do." While the war would continue for another year, Jenny began to correspond with Dan about postwar plans. His wartime letters had been strictly matter-of-fact, so much so that in a rare display of anger Jenny burned them. Two brief meetings when Dan was on furloughs had been strained. Recently, however, he had written a letter with an entirely different tone.

> I like the photograph of the Taos County Farmer's Union
> delegates. It is one of the best pictures of you I've seen.
> You have changed. You are leaner and your eyes are
> alert and your features determined. I can see the change
> in your life is already apparent in your appearance and
> your bearing. . . . Besides all this, you are lovely, lovelier
> than I've seen you in years—or maybe I haven't seen you
> in years. I don't know, but I should suspect that it is a

combination of the two: you are lovelier, and I am seeing you in a new light. (And I like the light so much.)

Jenny in turn wrote to her mother.

> I am convinced that whatever came between Dan and me—and it was something very intangible—was more than half my blame. I've had a wonderful opportunity to learn a few things about myself, and one is that I've always been too dependent on Dan—not exactly a weight around his neck, or a ball and chain—but I haven't been an individual contributing my share to our relationship. I think that is why Dan is so happy about my work in the Farmers Union. I came to that all on my own and found a place for myself as an individual, not as someone's wife.... That's why our next meeting will be so important, and time will be much too short to catch up with each other. I don't think that the catching up is going to be only my job, for Dan has to catch up with me, too, and it's the first time that has been so.

Finally acknowledging the rift between her and Dan, Jenny still withheld the real reason for it. And while she continued to hold herself partially responsible for the estrangement, the letter to her mother is revealing for its expression of newfound self-confidence. She was willing to attempt reconciliation, but she expected to be met halfway. She was right about something else. Her next meeting with Dan would be critical—and it would not be in New Mexico. He still held academic aspirations, and after his discharge wanted to live in New York. So in September 1945 Jenny left San Cristobal, not knowing if she would ever be back.

Starting Over

Hello, Larry! Jenny wrote: "I am living in a tall building—nine stories tall—right near the water. 'The house I live in' is all on the ninth floor. Dr. and Mrs. Curran (whom I call Jean and Frances) are good friends of Gaga. Jean knew me when I was a tiny baby.... I drove into New York City early Sunday morning."

Leaving New Mexico, Jenny had dropped Larry off with her in-laws in Wisconsin. East of Chicago she picked up a solitary soldier who was hitchhiking home to Pittsburgh and drove him all the way to his door. She was happy to help out a returning GI and to have some company for a while. But as she drove on toward New York Jenny knew she would finish the trip alone. She had 350 miles to go and three difficult years to mull over. The only company she wanted now was the sound of the postwar big bands and velvety crooners that poured from the radio.

In Brooklyn Jenny stayed with the Currans while she looked for an apartment of her own. Jean, now head of a medical school on Long Island, was the former Carleton College student who taught Jenny the rooster song. Soon Jenny auditioned for the American Theatre Wing War Service, the organization of stage, radio, screen, vaudeville, and music professionals that provided voluntary entertainment to veterans recovering in area hospitals, as well as for such local impresarios as Barney Josephson of Café Society and Max Gordon of the Village Vanguard. She briefly landed a job playing the piano in a hotel cocktail lounge, but walked away from it when she learned it was a union position and she was, in effect, a scab.

The American Theatre Wing welcomed her immediately, and her frequent letters kept Larry up-to-date on her suddenly busy schedule.

> On Staten Island a Red Cross girl met me and took me out to an army hospital very much like the one in Santa Fe where I used to go ... the boys in this hospital are mostly from New York. Some were quite sick. They liked having entertainment on Thanksgiving Day. In another ward was a man who didn't speak English; he knew only French. I was happy to be able to sing him a French song, and his eyes just sparkled. Next Thursday I go to St. Albans, the Navy hospital. I have dates scattered all through December, including Christmas Eve and New Year's Eve.

Jenny's impact on the recovering soldiers was as dramatic as it had been at Bruns Hospital in Santa Fe. After one of her visits to a hospital in Northport, an aviator who had received the Congressional Medal of Honor responded for the first time since being admitted. In Wisconsin, Larry had a dream: "I was walking on the frozen lake way out when I saw Jenny on the shore, so I came in to get her and we walked way out together."

In January 1946 Jenny heard her idol in concert for the first time:

> Tuesday night I heard Paul Robeson in a very fine concert. It was the first time I'd heard him in a concert, and it exceeded all my joyous anticipation. Among his selections were "Water Boy" and "Deep River," and then

the "Peat Bog Soldiers," a Red Army song, and "Joe Hill." He got a tremendous ovation by a packed house.

By the mid-1940s Robeson was one of the most famous men in the world. An academic and athletic star in college, a successful actor (within the limitations of roles offered a black man), and a singer of stunning power, Robeson was first and foremost a champion of the rights of all peoples. Singing for Allied troops during the war did not prevent him from being branded a threat to American democracy by those who feared his radical, anticolonialist politics. Jenny was thrilled to hear him sing Earl Robinson and Alfred Hayes's classic labor song, "Joe Hill."

Robeson was one of many luminaries—Aaron Copland and Leonard Bernstein among them—who sponsored a left-wing organization called People's Songs. People's Songs had been founded in December 1945 by a group of like-minded musicians and singers that included Pete Seeger, Woody Guthrie, Lee Hays, Millard Lampell, Arthur Stern, Agnes "Sis" Cunningham, Josh White, Peter Hawes, and Bess (Lomax) Hawes—the core of what would become the Almanac Singers and, later, the Weavers. Ronnie Gilbert and Irwin Silber were early members, and it wasn't long before Jenny joined them. The organization promoted music as a weapon for world peace, civil liberties, and human rights. While it would operate only three years before falling victim to the cold war, People's Songs would prove an important link between the prewar Old Left and the postwar New Left, particularly by its example of merging politics and music.

People's Songs also published a bulletin of the same name. In 1946 the inaugural issue optimistically declared, "The people are on the march and must have songs to sing." It was music to Jenny's ears. She was already a veteran union performer as well as a staunch advocate of the importance of music to political movements. The same month she attended Robeson's concert, she sang on the picket line for striking Western Union employees, and later was a welcomed performer at the union's victory party. She sang for a reunion of the Veterans of the Abraham Lincoln Brigade and for a Negro History Week rally at Local 65, an amalgam of unions headquartered on Astor Place in lower Manhattan. Her program there featured "The House I Live In," written by Earl Robinson and Lewis Allan, the latter the pen name of Abel Meeropol, who would adopt the orphaned sons of Julius and Ethel Rosenberg.

A union newspaper caught up with Jenny and published a glowing profile under the headline, "Wandering Minstrel—With a Union Label."

> A pretty girl with a broad, warm smile on her face and an accordion strapped across her shoulders walked out of the shadows to the center of the floor. The spotlight played on her colorful peasant skirt as she stepped in front of the mike to announce her first song. She paused, adjusted her accordion and started to sing. "... The house I live in ... my neighbors White and Black ... the people who've just come here ... or from generations back ... "
>
> The applause rolled out and kept on rolling. . . .
> To put it mildly, she brought the house down.
>
> This was the first Club 65 appearance of a girl who traveled 3,000 miles from a ranch in New Mexico to entertain Union members in New York.
>
> Recently, we met the gal with the voice and the accordion. She is Jeannette Wells, who for the past five months has been singing for trade unionists throughout the city. . . .
>
> Jeannette is a hit and it's no wonder. In addition to a fine voice, she sings the kind of songs Union members enjoy; songs that tell a story, like "The House I Live In" and "Joe Hill." She sings folk songs of many countries, Negro spirituals, and songs of current significance.

"I'm knee-deep in this kind of work," she wrote Larry, "as well as the hospitals, and life is full."

Full, yet empty. Jenny's confidence as a performer was growing, yet something was missing. Months of singing for recovering veterans probably lifted her spirits as much as it did theirs, but it could not remove entirely the pain of her loneliness. There were days when she felt like she was moving through a fog, one of the wounded herself. In February 1946 she wrote to Larry, "Do you know that you and Dan and I have never been together as a family? All by ourselves." Finally, word came from Dan in Ft. Ord, California: he was being discharged and would pick up Larry on his way to New York.

"At this moment I don't know which baffles me more," she wrote her mother-in-law, "the prospect of being a good mother or a good wife. I want so much to be both, and I feel so out of step." At the end of another lonesome day in March she returned home with still no word. Practically in tears, she lay down and fell asleep. At six she rose to prepare her dinner. The doorbell rang four times—usually the phone signal—so she casually looked out the door. Coming down the hall were Larry in a red jacket and cap and Dan close behind. "Such joy I have never before felt, absolute complete joy and excitement. Larry came right up to me, and I picked him up and hugged him, then dashed to Dan." At the end of March 1946 she cabled her in-laws, "Dan Larry Jennie trucks books bicycle happily settled down Love."

It lasted three weeks. For that brief moment, the Wells family was together. Dan landed a job with Win the Peace, an organization dedicated to good relations between the United States and the Soviet Union, and suddenly he was gone all the time, traveling for the group. He never again lived in the apartment on any regular basis. Jenny concealed her new sadness in letters home: "Larry and I don't see much of him, but it's wonderful to have him happy in his work, and it is what he needed."

Larry retained his characteristic resilience. Sunny mornings might find him outside swinging on a railing and singing "O What a Beautiful Morning," a song Jenny had taught him from Rodgers and Hammerstein's *Oklahoma!* Jenny continued to perform. She appeared with the George Brockman/Alice Dudley Dance Group for a Russian relief benefit, at Local 65's annual convention, and at an American Labor Party meeting. At a later ALP event she shared the stage for the first time with Seeger and Guthrie. Jenny played again with Seeger at a People's Songs hootenanny as well as at a Boston hootenanny that also featured Guthrie, Sonny Terry, and Brownie McGhee. She remained a regular at Club 65, a nightclub operated by Local 65, where she appeared with Guthrie and Hazel Scott. At the same time, the Red Cross asked her to come back to the hospitals, where the veterans adored her renditions of such popular songs as "Old Black Magic" and "Don't Fence Me In."

One evening, after singing at a fundraising event for Win the Peace, a young man asked her name. Jeannette Wells, she said, Dan is my husband. Oh, he replied, I thought Dan's wife had dark hair. It was not long after that event that Jenny was awakened after midnight by a knock on her door. Throwing on a robe, she cautiously opened the door. Standing before her was Dan. She had not seen him for weeks. His eyes met hers and he said, "I can't keep it to myself any longer."

Once he started he couldn't stop. Earlier that evening Dan had attended Arthur Miller's play *All My Sons*, a drama about the emotional damage caused by family members who conceal things from each other. He got on the subway and came over to the apartment to make a clean breast of it. His affair with Joan had continued uninterrupted these past four years. When he was in New York, working odd jobs while waiting to be called into the service, he was living with Joan. After he was inducted into the army, he continued to see Joan. When he left Jenny and Larry again, after only three weeks in New York, he returned to Joan. In fact, he and Joan had seen *All My Sons* together. The whole story poured out in one sudden catharsis—all except for that first rendezvous in Kansas City. Dan never mentioned it.

Jenny felt like the floor was collapsing under her feet. All during the difficult period in New York, before Dan arrived and then when they were together only infrequently, she had remained faithful to him. Not only had Dan been unfaithful, he had betrayed her in public. Some of her friends considered her devotion naive and foolish, but the fact was she still loved him. The humiliation and anger that Jenny had struggled to submerge now returned. Dan was in the apartment less than an hour, asked for a divorce, and left. It would be some time before she learned that when he drove east he had not only picked up Larry but stopped in Chicago for Joan. He made Larry promise not to mention her. While it was unlikely that Larry grasped the situation, Dan had made him an unwitting accomplice. Jenny never forgave that.

On March 10, 1947, Deborah Ferry noted in her diary, "Had a letter from Jenny this afternoon, saying she was leaving Dan. We were not surprised. Wish it had happened years ago. She and Larry left Brooklyn yesterday." In San Cristobal, Fran and Fred Gunther awaited her arrival. When Jenny got home she discovered that she and Dan were not the only couple having problems. Fred was not treating Fran well: he did not encourage her in any of her interests and he absolutely refused when she wanted to adopt a child. What neither Fran nor Jenny had recognized, at least at the outset, was that Fred was homosexual. "That was quite a summer," Jenny says. "We cried on each other's shoulders and supported each other at the same time."

The day Jenny's divorce became final, in June 1947, she performed for the first time at the University of New Mexico in Albuquerque. UNM sociologist Lyle Saunders had met Jenny through mutual friends, and it was Saunders who suggested to his colleague Joaquin Ortega, head of the School of Inter-American Affairs, that Jenny be invited to present a bilingual concert at the university. Her debut was so successful that she returned the following year and shared the stage with Pete Seeger and Manuel Archuleta of San Juan Pueblo. The event was important in reintroducing her to the southwestern audience after two years in New York, and a discovery that occurred as a result of the concert would have a lasting impact on Jenny's life.

Saunders and Ortega told her about an archive of north-ern New Mexico music that had been gathering dust in a library basement since it was first transcribed over ten years earlier. Jenny inquired at UNM's Zimmerman Library only to discover that the materials were missing. She checked around Albuquerque and learned that a branch library out on Central Avenue had a copy of the archive. Helpful librarians made a complete copy of it for her at no charge. When she got home, Jenny was taken aback by the trea-sure trove of song and story she had before her.

Long before she left San Cristobal for New York, Jenny had begun the serious study of Spanish-language folk music. Her methods were simple. She kept a series of little notebooks—cuadernitos—labeled "United States," "Mexico," "South America," "Asia/Pacific," even "Miscellaneous," into which she jotted down songs according to their country of origin. If a neighbor played a waltz that she admired, Jenny asked him to teach it to her. If some-one asked her if she knew a particular song, she would scour song-books until she located it. She might have saved some time by using a typewriter, but just as she revered the immediacy of folk music in performance she did not want anything to come between her and the intimacy of writing out lyrics and notation.

What she now had in her hands was a collection that had been compiled in 1936 and 1937 under the auspices of the New Deal's Works Progress Administration. The archive comprised four man-uscripts with an introduction by A. L. Campa, then director of research in folklore and a professor of modern languages at the uni-versity. "The symphonic epic of America will be composed of songs that include every region and particularly those regions whose traditions date beyond the settlements on the eastern shores," he wrote. "We are not dealing with a revival of obsolete material but, rather, with a preservation of something that is alive today."

Campa might have been surprised to learn that this mate-rial would find some of its greatest expression in the hands of a Midwestern Anglo with a Vassar College education. The first vol-ume contained children's songs, singing games, and sayings. The second and third were given to folk songs in Spanish with English translations. What particularly caught Jenny's eye was volume four. It contained thirty dance melodies transcribed and arranged by Aurelio Armendariz. Some of them form the core of Jenny's repertoire to this day.

Following their respective divorces, Jenny and Fran decided to get away from the ranch for a while. There were too many ghosts there at the moment. They rented a cottage on Caroline Street in Albuquerque that was convenient to a public school for Larry. Fran adopted a baby girl from the Tesuque Pueblo, secured a full-time teaching job, and was on her way to a restored self-image. Jenny, however, was still coming to grips with what had happened in New York. "It is unbelievable to most people that I was there for almost two years before I found out what was going on," she says. "But I knew that Dan had to work things out, even if I didn't know exactly what he was doing. I never knew where he was living. He occasionally showed up when he needed money, and his relationship with Larry was superficial."

In October 1947 Jenny drove to Chicago to visit her family and attend a People's Songs convention at Hull House. There she met Jessie O'Connor. Neither knew anything about the other, but they struck up a warm acquaintance. When they said their good-byes at the end of the convention, they learned to their surprise that they each were going on to Winnetka, where in fact both of them had grown up.

When Jenny told her parents about meeting Jessie, Frank Ferry was visibly amused. Jessie O'Connor, he said, is the former Jessie Lloyd—an heiress to the *Chicago Tribune* fortune; granddaughter of Henry Demarest Lloyd, a nineteenth-century social reformer and author of *Wealth Against the World*, a denunciation of the oil industry; and daughter of William Bross Lloyd, the "Winnetka socialist." She was married to Harvey O'Connor, a devoted socialist and Wobbly (member of the Industrial Workers of the World). Harvey was eastern bureau manager of Federated Press, a labor news service, and Jessie was already established as a labor journalist.

Meeting Jessie O'Connor thrust Jenny's leftwing politics into the Ferry household conversation, an event as rare as uttering the name Roosevelt. One evening Frank, Frank Jr., and Jenny had a discussion on communism during which Jenny said, "Dad, as long as we have a cousin younger than I am who has so much money that he doesn't know what to do with it and so is drinking himself into an early grave, and I have a neighbor in New Mexico who died in childbirth because she couldn't get medical help, then something is wrong with the way things are in this country." Frank responded with a mischievous twinkle in his eye, "Jenny, you're a communist and don't even know it!"

She did, of course. So did the FBI. By this time the bureau had opened a file on Deborah Jeannette Hill Wells. On another occasion when someone asked Jenny if she was a communist she answered that she was a *communalist*. "Born that way, always been that way." The distinction is important and cannot be dismissed by flippant claims that all communists—or members of any party, for that matter—are carbon copies of each other. Party membership notwithstanding, Jenny was a communist with a small "c."

There were many like her. Neither party polemicists nor radical recruiters, these people moved within a broad swath of leftist organizations and ideas. Jenny's brand of communitarian politics really resembled classic Progressivism, a short-lived (roughly 1900–1914) movement but one that informs the left to this day. Progressivism was born as a response to the late-nineteenth-century explosion of unregulated industrialism, mass immigration, and the nation's rapid shift from an agrarian to an urban society. Progressives like Jenny believe in human dignity and take it for granted that human intelligence can remake society for the benefit of all. To that end they advocate not the overthrow of their government but its reform.

The People's Songs convention was enlightening for Jenny, but more importantly the family reunion dispelled any lingering estrangement between her and her mother over Jenny's inability to confide in her about her troubles with Dan. Earlier that year, Frank Ferry had written Jenny and admonished her gently for the "chip on your shoulder when you have stated your political opinions about certain subjects." He reminded her that "you should have been able to come to your mother for love and sympathy during the tough period you have been passing through. I think she was hurt that so many people knew about your trouble before she did."

After a week in Illinois Jenny returned to the little house in Albuquerque. For the first time in many years, she had time on her hands. Her days were not taken up from dawn to dark with cooking, cleaning, teaching, farming, and the thousand and one other tasks that had consumed her while operating a summer camp and a school. Now, at the end of 1947, Jenny sat down and took stock of herself.

At age thirty-four, she was a divorcee and a single mother. She had devoted thirteen years to her husband and their vision of a ranch and school. Now her husband was gone, the school shut down, and the ranch closed indefinitely. She did not know if she would return to it. Her emotions were raw, but she could see that the world was not entirely collapsing around her. Larry was doing well in school. Fran was teaching in Albuquerque and had a new man in her life, Joe DiSanti. Jenny remained true to her character—solid and straightforward, more given to action than analysis. Music was her anchor. She enjoyed performing in public and had known some success, but did not want to be away from Larry. So as this turbulent year in her life drew to a close, Jenny settled on a compromise. She would continue her music, but be selective as to when and where she performed so as not to be an absentee parent for any length of time.

Jenny's plans were no more definite than this when she received devastating news. In January 1948 Frank Ferry died at the age of sixty-eight. His health had been faltering in recent months; he fell back from the dinner table one night and was gone. At his memorial service, Jenny heard many testimonials to him and realized how many people shared her own high opinion of him. "The innate dignity of his person and his quiet ways marked every aspect of his life," said one friend. Another added: "Many turned to Mr. Ferry for advice and counsel. He saw things with clarity of mind and depth of understanding, and could use his noble imagination and sensitive feeling so that whatever he gave his attention to had wisdom and goodness in it."

Back in Albuquerque Jenny kept recalling scenes from her childhood. There was Dad, inventing games with her at the pool table. There was Dad on the balcony where he smoked his cigars and flipped the ends into the snow—only to have spring reveal a disgusting collection of decomposed butts. There was Dad in his garden. Everything he touched grew, whether in business or in the garden. The words of one eulogizer played over and over in her mind: Frank knew how to take the time to make up his mind and find the way to judicious decisions. Facing yet another turning point in her life, Jenny would take those words to heart and try to live up to the example set by her stepfather. In the middle of her deliberations came a note from Sarah Tepping in Denver. "Come for a visit: There is someone I want you to meet."

Hill family portrait, Northfield, Minnesota,
c. 1915. Standing: Deborah Sayles Hill,
Mary Hill. Seated: Bob, Fred Burnett Hill,
Jenny, Ned, and Fred Jr. (Bud).

Ferry/Hill family portrait, Winnetka, Illinois,
1924 or 1925. Standing: Fred Burnett "Bud"
Hill Jr., Frank Ferry. Seated: Jenny, Deborah
Hill Ferry, Frank Ferry Jr., Mary Hill.
Below: Ned Hill, Bob Hill.

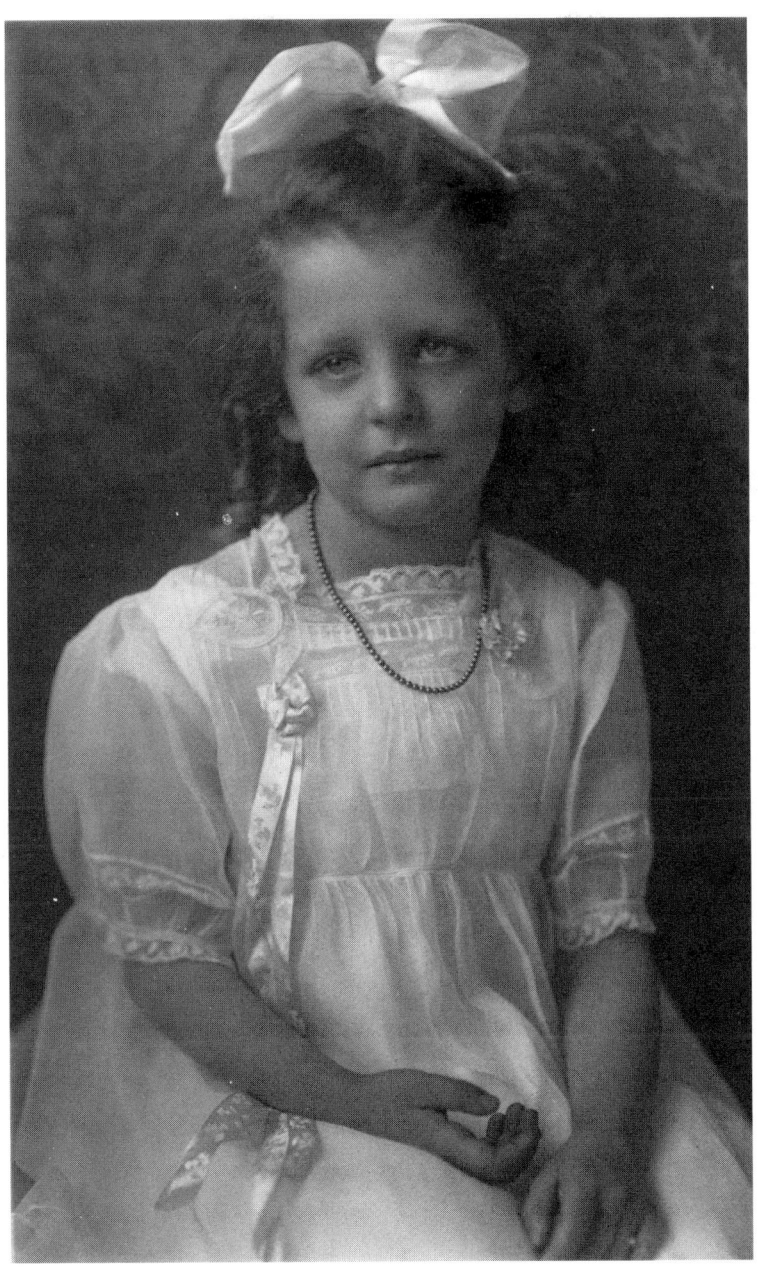

Jenny at age four or five.

The 1934 Vassar field hockey team,
Jenny front row center.

Jenny and Dan Wells on their wedding day,
June 20, 1934, Winnetka, Illinois.

Jenny and Dan on the Lawrence Trek,
Mary Queen of Scots Tower, England, 1935.

Jenny drawing water at the
D. H. Lawrence cottage,
Cornwall, England, 1935.

ABOVE: Angelo Ravagli (back to camera), Jenny (with camera), Frieda Lawrence, Karl Hilton (in cap), and Fran Wells at Frieda's Kiowa Ranch, San Cristobal, New Mexico, 1937.

RIGHT: Chores at San Cristobal Valley Ranch, c. 1940. No one had any trouble falling asleep at the end of a long day.

ABOVE:
Rev. Glyn Patrick
Smith, J. Amarante
Martinez, Jenny,
J. B. Rael, and
Marcelino Martinez
at Rocky Mountain
Farmers Union
convention, Denver,
1943 or 1944.

LEFT: Rufina Baca
with children of the
Valdez School.
In the 1940s Baca
first brought Jenny
in to sing for her
students, defying
the ban on the use
of Spanish in the
classroom.

SIX

Amor Ardiente

His name was Craig Vincent, and he was executive secretary of something called the Rocky Mountain Council for Social Action, a nonprofit organization dedicated to improving conditions for the underprivileged in the Denver area. Craig and Sarah were friends, and when he mentioned that the council had scheduled a fundraiser in February featuring Pete Seeger but would like to showcase regional musicians as well, Sarah smiled. "I know just the person for you," she said. There was no telephone yet in the house in Albuquerque; Jenny and Fran were temporarily using a pay phone at a nearby gas station. Sarah got the number from Jenny and arranged for Craig to call at 7:00 PM one night. When Jenny picked it up, the voice that came over the line was a warm antidote to a crisp winter evening.

Jenny told Craig that she was already scheduled to give several concerts in the Denver area in early February and was planning to stay with Sarah. She said she knew Seeger from New York and would be pleased to join him at the council event. The day before she was to perform in Boulder, Jenny drove to Sarah's house. Craig Vincent was there. Jenny told him she would be in Boulder tomorrow but back at Sarah's the following day. When she returned, Sarah was bursting to talk. Craig is very interested in you, she said. He wants to know all about you. He's coming over.

Jenny did not resist. Craig Vincent was a political activist; he was also strikingly handsome with warm blue eyes, an easy sense of humor, and a charming, understated sophistication. That night he escorted Jenny to her concert at Denver University. Afterward, he invited Jenny to go dancing. He knew of a good swing band playing at a hotel in a black neighborhood in Denver. The following day, Craig picked her up for the Rocky Mountain Council fundraiser, where she saw a lot of people she knew. Jenny and Pete Seeger each performed solo, then sang together on several political songs.

Seeger was scheduled to play the next day at a Progressive Party benefit for Henry Wallace, who recently had announced his third-party campaign for president, and he asked Jenny to join him. It was a whirlwind of a week, but it all fit together. Craig was also head of the Progressive Party in Colorado, so with Seeger's invitation Jenny lingered in Denver through February 17, Craig's birthday. "That was the beginning," Jenny says. "It really was chemistry."

Craig made a point of telling Jenny two things right away. First, he also was a member of the Communist Party. Second, he was not yet divorced from his wife, although they were long separated and she lived on the East Coast. Jenny and Craig could commiserate together about their first marriages. By the time Jenny returned to Albuquerque, the uncertainty of only a month before had vanished. Her concerts had been successful and her appearances at the council fundraiser and campaign event had opened broader political horizons to her. Most important, she was falling in love. "Craig was very affectionate, very attentive," Jenny says. "I think he missed this kind of intimacy in his marriage, as I had in mine. Craig brought out the earthiness in me. I learned a lot from Dan, but in Craig my heart and soul came together."

There is no apolitical act. This was the Law According to Craig. One of four sons of a prolabor lawyer, Craig graduated from

Grand Junction (Colorado) High School and Stanford University. He studied law at Denver University Law School and was elected to the Colorado State Legislature in 1932, the same year that swept Franklin Roosevelt into the White House. Craig was a Democrat, but the defining word on his campaign flyers was "progressive." He advocated unemployment insurance, the abolition of child labor, a graduated income tax, and reduced government costs.

He was not in the legislature long before he was appointed state director of the national re-employment service. In 1939 Craig married Joyce Campbell. Joyce would later work with Anna Rosenberg, a government labor specialist who became the target of a McCarthy smear campaign in 1950 after Secretary of State George Marshall nominated her to be an assistant secretary. She was cleared and confirmed but the tactics used against her, including paid informers, made a lasting impression on Craig and would haunt him and Jenny in the future.

In 1942 Craig was appointed Atlantic Coast regional representative of the Recruitment and Manning Organization (RMO) in the War Shipping Administration. He was in the job little more than a year when a controversy erupted over proposed integration of living quarters aboard ships. In an issue of *Seafarer's Log*, published by the Seafarers International Union (SIU), a front-page photo of Craig appeared under the headline, "EXPOSED! This photo is proof of a fact well known to seamen—Craig Vincent, New York head of the RMO, is a fellow-traveler of the Communist Party. He is shown here addressing, on Sept. 14, 1941, a mass meeting sponsored by the 'citizens' Committee Against Police Brutality in Washington, D.C. This 'committee' was a Stalinist front organization, and you can bet that slick Mr. Vincent was no innocent that was sucked in." In the same issue, columnist Matthew Dushane accused the National Maritime Union (NMU) of being infiltrated with communists. "The rumors are that RMO's regional director in New York, Mr. Craig Vincent, is the cheer leader for the NMU, and has been pushing the commie line on discrimination and is trying to compel the SUP and the SIU to checker-board their crews."

Dushane's term "checker-board" exposed the real issue at

stake—not politics but race. The SIU sent a letter to Congressman Howard Smith accusing Craig of pushing the union to abandon its policy that white seamen not be forced to eat and sleep in the same quarters with "Negro" seamen. In 1940 Smith, a conservative Democrat, had sponsored the Smith Act, which made it illegal to advocate or teach the forcible overthrow of the government or to belong to a group advocating or teaching such action. During subsequent hearings Craig insisted that he followed the rule of first-come-first-served when assigning recruits to ships. "Do you favor social intermingling of races?" asked Rep. Clare Hoffman (R., Mich.). "Yes," said Craig, "if the people want to intermingle." Even Craig's declaration that he believed in free enterprise could not deflect the attacks that this brought down on him.

Ultimately, the president's Fair Employment Practice Committee directed the SIU to hire seamen without regard to race, creed, or color. Craig had made enemies, but his mail also brought messages of support. One correspondent wrote, "We must realize that the real radicals in our country are those who don't wish to look upon such a solution. I'm worried about it because unless we can get more ranking persons to express themselves as you have, a new war *will* come to America." As he left the administration in 1945, Craig wrote his supervisor, "I expect to go out to Colorado for a few weeks, and entertain the idea of staying there if possible—meaning getting a job that will permit pork chops on the table and political activity as a side dish." It was vintage Vincent tongue-in-cheek. For Craig, politics would always be the main course.

In April 1948 Craig came to Albuquerque to meet Larry, and they hit it off immediately. In June, Jenny and Larry traveled to Illinois, an occasion that provided some amusing political moments. At the same time Deborah Ferry was listening to the radio as the Republican Party nominated New York Governor Thomas Dewey for the presidency, Jenny was on the south side of Chicago singing for Henry Wallace.

The fascinating confrontation in the watershed presidential election of 1948 was not between Dewey and incumbent President Harry Truman but between Truman and Wallace. These two men shared rural, Midwestern backgrounds and political careers begun in the New Deal. But the similarities stopped there. At the end of the war, when publisher Henry Luce spoke of the coming "American century," Wallace retorted with the "century of the common man." Yet he was anything but common. He had been a plant geneticist, farm journalist, secretary of agriculture (his father had held the same post), and vice president during Franklin Roosevelt's third term. He was pushed aside by his own party in favor of Truman, and when FDR died in 1945 it is small wonder that Wallace considered Truman a White House usurper.

Wallace stayed on as secretary of commerce, but when he continued to address foreign affairs, in particular his outspoken support of good relations with the Soviet Union, Truman fired him. Wallace was deluged with mail lamenting his dismissal. Albert Einstein wrote, "Your courageous intervention deserves the gratitude of all of us who observe the present attitude of our government with grave concern." "Rejoicing, I watch you faring forth on a renewed pilgrimage," wrote Helen Keller.

Wallace launched his renewed pilgrimage in December 1947 when he announced that he would be the Progressive Party candidate for president. America, however, was now two years into the cold war, and much of the country demonstrated little patience with those like Wallace who advocated extending the olive branch to Moscow.

In the spring of 1948 Jenny presented folk song programs at Texas Christian University and to public school children in Terrell, Texas. She stayed in Forth Worth with Harvey and Jessie O'Connor, who arranged for her to perform at a Progressive Party campaign rally in Tyler and a Students-for-Wallace event at Southern Methodist University. Jenny's political repertoire included "Union Maid," "Keep Your Hand on the Plow, Hold On" (later adapted as the

Civil Rights–era anthem "Keep Your Eyes on the Prize, Hold On"), as well as "The Same Merry-Go-Round," a novelty song written for the Wallace campaign by Ray Glazer and Bill Wolff.

> The donkey is tired and thin,
> the elephant thinks he'll move in;
> they yell and they fuss but they ain't foolin' us,
> 'cause they're brothers right under the skin.

> It's the same, same merry-go-round.
> Which one will you ride this year?
> the donkey and elephant bob up and down
> on the same merry-go-round.

Although election campaign songs tend to share the longevity of election campaign promises, they played a central role in the Wallace movement, which at times could resemble a revival meeting complete with sound trucks and singers. Jenny's contribution in this regard was significant, both at the convention and on the road. Tyler, Texas, however, was a case-in-point for the difficulties the Progressives encountered in 1948.

In March the town turned a cold shoulder on a Wallace campaign organizational meeting. The *Tyler Courier-Times* reported that only three people turned out. "That is about the way that Wallace rates all over the South," the paper editorialized, "and we believe that that is about the way the Wallace-Appeasement-of-Russia Program rates all over the United States." When the candidate issued a peace proposal for the United States and Russia, a letter to which Joseph Stalin replied favorably, a cartoon in the Tyler paper blasted him as "Little RED Riding Wallace," standing naively by the bedside of a Russian bear disguised as grandma. A subsequent editorial read, "He may be confused and misled, as he has been in the past, but the fact remains that he has accepted the support of a political party that puts its loyalty to Moscow first." In Texas and elsewhere, it was not uncommon for Wallace campaign organizers to find their houses splashed with red paint.

In the summer of 1948, Wallace visited Jenny and Craig in San Cristobal during a western campaign swing. One afternoon, he wandered off into the fields behind the main house with Joe Santisteven, a young ranch hand. When he saw that the land was planted with crested wheat, Wallace pointed to it proudly and said it was during his tenure as secretary of agriculture that the wheat was brought to this area. Wallace spent a week in San Cristobal, met with the tribal council at Taos Pueblo, spoke on Taos Plaza, and played baseball at the ranch. As a parting gift Wallace, who spoke some Spanish and was interested in Mexico and South America, gave Jenny a typewritten collection of folk song lyrics in Spanish with English translations. Jenny continues to perform several songs from this collection. He also gave her an autographed baseball, which she treasures.

This summer was an extraordinary one for Jenny, both politically and musically. She fulfilled a lifelong dream when she accompanied Paul Robeson at a Progressive Party rally in Colorado. Robeson's regular accompanist, pianist Larry Brown, had not traveled with him, so Jenny was tapped to back up the singer. She had learned a great deal by observing Robeson, especially the ease with which he moved in and out of languages in international folk song and his attention to such details as the provenance and composers of songs. Still, "I have never shaken like that in my life!" she recalls. "We had no time to rehearse, so he handed me his sheet music, then turned to the audience and said, 'Jenny and I didn't have time to practice, but we'll do the best we can.' Of course I more or less anticipated what he would sing—his program included 'The House I Live In,' 'There's a Man Going 'Round Taking Names,' and some spirituals—but I had to transpose keys a number of times." After the performance Robeson turned to her and said, 'You certainly gave me great backup.'" If only my mother could see me now, Jenny thought.

In July Jenny and Craig attended the Progressive Party convention in Philadelphia. For Jenny, it was a heady experience. It was her first—and would be her only—performance at a major political party nominating convention, and she shared the stage with Pete

Seeger and Senator Glen Taylor, the party's candidate for vice president. Robeson sang on another day.

Jenny was still shy about openly accompanying Craig. ("Jenny is traveling with a married man!" her sister Mary protested to their mother, but Deborah Ferry said, "Jenny is a grown woman. She knows what she's doing.") So after the convention Jenny and Craig traveled to introduce each other to their respective families. In her diary, Deborah Ferry noted, "They drove in about 4:45, tired after constant driving for three or four days.... We had a nice visit with Jenny & Craig late this evening. They told us all about the Wallace convention. They have stickers on their car which say 'Work with Wallace.' We liked Craig in spite of his politics." Jenny's brothers split their verdict: one refused to meet Craig, saying he was a communist, but another did, talking sports with him until one in the morning. This would remain a pattern for Craig Vincent's relationships. Throughout his life even those who stood at opposite ends of the political spectrum would find him charming, reasonable, and a man of wide interests.

Charges of communist infiltration haunted Henry Wallace's campaign. In fact, the 1948 Progressive Party was not a communist creation but a merger of several leftist organizations, and the communists at first were hesitant to join. When they did get on the bandwagon they came on strong. Principled and impractical, Wallace either could not or would not refuse their support. Constant negative publicity helped unravel his campaign, and Truman began to lure away liberals by adapting parts of the Progressive message. Wallace was left to doggedly pursue his mission—and dodge the increasing numbers of eggs, tomatoes, and firecrackers that greeted him at campaign stops.

In the end, he polled only slightly more than one million popular votes to finish last behind Truman, Dewey, and Dixiecrat Strom Thurmond. He did not carry a single state. The American visionary who had in his lifetime been a Republican, a Democrat, a Progressive, secretary of agriculture, secretary of commerce, and vice president of the United States retired to his farm in Westchester, New York. In 1952, Wallace lunched in Washington with political columnist Drew Pearson, who later noted in his diary, "Wallace opened up at lunch in a very frank way about the third-party movement. He realizes now how the communists used him."

For Jenny and Craig and many like-minded liberals, the Wallace debacle seemed like the last gasp of the Roosevelt New Deal era and perhaps of the Old Left itself. They returned to San Cristobal, ready as always to remain active, but now on the local level. For them a personal milestone lay ahead. In January 1949, they were married in Reno, Nevada, with Deborah Ferry as witness. Jenny and Craig met her mother at the train station and took her to the Riverside Hotel. The next morning she and Jenny ran errands in Woolworth's, "where the clerks all called us 'honey' or 'darling.' J remarked that she had never been so honeyed in her life." That evening, Craig gave Deborah a tour of casino row along Virginia Street, and the following day he and Jenny were married in a private ceremony—the details of which would soon find their way into Jenny's FBI file.

Back in Taos, Jenny was in a grocery store on the plaza one day, talking with a Mr. Oliver, the butcher, when Dorothy Brett walked in. When Jenny told Brett that she had remarried, Brett, who was quite deaf, reared back and roared, "Well, what did you get this time?"

SEVEN

Salt of the Earth

"Holiday in Northern New Mexico!" In the spring of 1949 Jenny and Craig reopened her San Cristobal property as a guest ranch and placed advertisements in such leftist publications as the *People's Daily World* and the *National Guardian*: "San Cristobal Valley Ranch, located eighteen miles from Taos. Unusual recreation and cultural program featuring Earl Robinson. Weekly rates. Interracial." The ads no sooner appeared than attacks from the right wing followed. An article in the July 29, 1949, issue of *Counterattack*, a part gossip, part conspiracy newsletter founded by ex-FBI agents, blasted Jenny and Craig as "Commugressives" and the ranch as a resort that combined fun with Commugressive propaganda.

In December Jenny performed at a People's Songs concert in New York, after which she and Craig traveled to Illinois where Larry was staying with Dan's parents. Jenny eagerly anticipated a Christmas reunion with Fran and Joe DiSanti, who had married the year before and were due to arrive from Salt Lake City. What Jenny did not know was that the Wellses had planned a full—and surprise—family reunion. When Dan and Joan walked in the tension was palpable. Jenny, Craig, and Larry soon left to stay with Deborah Ferry. It had been two years since Larry had seen his father. Dan would return to San Cristobal only once, to collect some personal belongings. Neither Jenny nor Larry ever saw him again.

Early in 1950 an obscure senator from Wisconsin, looking for something that would vault him into prominence (and improve his re-election chances), latched onto an issue not of his own making but on which he would become the national demagogue. On February 9 Joseph McCarthy delivered a speech to the Women's Republican Club of Wheeling, West Virginia, during which he told his audience that he had a list of 205 communists that were working in the State Department. He had no such list, but it didn't seem to matter. Many in the press were as eager to find sensational news as McCarthy was to fabricate it. In these early days of the cold war, Americans were reeling from the Alger Hiss case, the fall of China to Mao's communists, and the announcement of the Russian atomic bomb. The country was primed for conspiracy theories, and McCarthy jumped on the Red Scare bandwagon that had been percolating since the Truman administration and made it his own.

That summer a man calling himself Harvey Matt stopped at San Cristobal Valley Ranch on his way to the West Coast. While there, he offered to be the social director for the ranch's popular Saturday night community events and did call at least one square dance on August 1. Jenny remembers Matt as a good dance caller and a talented man, but she and Craig took an immediate dislike to him because of his overbearing personality. In fact, Matt and the Vincents had crossed paths before, at the People's Songs event in New York the previous December.

What Jenny did not know was that Harvey Matt was really Harvey Matusow, an informer for the FBI. After serving in World War II, Matusow had returned to his native New York City where, after a year's postwar idleness, he joined the Communist Party. In 1948 he registered at the Jefferson School of Social Science, a Marxist adult education institute in New York associated with the Communist Party (and where, coincidentally, Dan Wells would later teach). Matusow stuffed envelopes for the Wallace campaign but afterward became disillusioned with the political left. Matusow was searching for self-importance and a sense of belonging. More than anything else, he wanted to be center stage. Envious of the attention lavished on such ex-communist informers as Whittaker Chambers and Elizabeth Bentley, Matusow contacted the FBI. "It was the easy way up," he later wrote, "to let the world know that I was not just another guy."

At the time he saw Jenny perform in 1949, Matusow was working at People's Songs, where his scheme for a book-and-record-buying club would saddle the already financially troubled organization with additional debt. When he showed up at Jenny's ranch in a red pickup truck weighted down with leftist literature he planned to sell in San Francisco, Matusow was on his way to a flamboyant, if brief, career as a paid informer and professional witness.

He stayed at the ranch one week, time enough for him to contribute information to Jenny's FBI file, which the bureau had been expanding with details on her personal and family background from such sources as the Winnetka Glencoe Credit Association, the Vassar College Recorder's Office, and the Washoe County (Reno) Recorder's Office. The FBI also regularly filed reports from numerous confidential sources like Matusow who would be identified as being of "known" or "unknown" reliability. A great many undemocratic practices were employed to investigate so-called threats to democracy.

Matusow supplied names and information about ranch guests to the FBI's Albuquerque office. After he left the ranch, Matusow remained in the Taos area for several months working at odd jobs including, apparently, occasional gofer for Frieda Lawrence and Mabel Dodge Luhan. All the while he continued to provide names, license plate numbers, and other information to the FBI. He also enrolled under the G.I. Bill at the Taos Valley Art School, operated by Louis Ribak. Ribak had emigrated from Russia and achieved artistic success in New York City before moving to New Mexico with his wife, Bea Mandelman. Matusow would brand Ribak a communist and contribute to the demise of the art school.

⊢◇⊣

In October 1950, miners from Local 890 of the International Union of Mine, Mill, and Smelter Workers (known as Mine Mill) walked out on strike in Hanover, in southern New Mexico's Grant County, against the Empire Zinc Corporation. Union organizer Clinton Jencks had overseen the merger of five separate locals into Local 890, and now the union struck for equal pay and treatment. Pay issues were only the tip of the iceberg. The miners were protesting a full range of inequities. Not only was there was a double-standard payroll at the mines, there were even separate windows where Anglos and Spanish-speaking workers picked up their checks. Anglos were paid more for softer jobs and lived in better conditions; Mexican and Mexican-American miners earned less for more dangerous work and lived in substandard housing without indoor plumbing.

In June 1951 a judge issued a restraining order giving the miners the choice of dismantling the strike or going to jail. One night, in a now legendary meeting, women—union wives and family, members of the Ladies Auxiliary—suggested they take over the picket line. Virginia Jencks, wife of Clinton Jencks and herself a veteran activist, Virginia Chacon, wife of union leader Juan Chacon, and others had spotted a loophole: the injunction referred only to officers, members, and agents of the union—in this case, all men. It was a historic, gender-bending proposition. At first the men resisted. They faced a seemingly no-win situation—give up the picket line, lose the strike; give up their jobs, lose them to scabs. Early in the morning, the women's motion carried.

Law enforcement officials and company goons responded with violence. The women were threatened, tear-gassed, and shot at, but would not yield. Strikebreakers drove into the lines, injuring several people including children. The women held firm. When they were jailed on false pretenses, they created such a commotion that the local sheriff released them. Their courage would be immortalized in a Mexican *corrido*, or narrative folk ballad, "El Corrido del Empire Zinc":

Pero la huelga no se acaba,
porque las mujeres valientes,
a los esquiroles golpeando,
estan ganado en todos frentes.

But the strike does not end,
because the brave women
are sticking it to the scabs,
they are winning on all fronts.

The company accused the strikers of being communists—in 1949 the CIO had expelled Mine Mill for being left-wing—but what drove the rank and file of Local 890 was not theoretical politics but realistic conditions.

Clinton and Virginia Jencks visited Jenny and Craig on several occasions during the strike. From Jenny's FBI file: "Confidential informant (name deleted) of known reliability, advises that (name deleted) International Organizer of the International Union of Mine, Mill and Smelter Workers at Bayard, New Mexico, has visited the San Cristobal Valley ranch several times in the past six months." Clint and Craig had known each other from earlier Colorado days, and now Craig and Jenny took great interest in the strike. "Jenny and Craig were both personable, wonderful people, always interested in union movements," Jencks said. "Jenny had a strong attraction to the Chicano movement at a time when there was a lot of discrimination against agricultural workers and Spanish-speaking peoples. She was rooted in the community, a woman interested in people as people."

As she had for the previous three years, Jenny sang for the 1951 Mine Mill convention, this time in Nogales, Arizona. According to Jenny's FBI file, the *March of Labor* would later credit Jenny with writing and performing "Viva la Mine and Mill," which became that convention's theme song. Jenny remembers also singing a ballad about Pancho Villa and his cavalry, the *dorados*, or golden ones, "De Los Dorados de Pancho Villa," with her own translation.

Yo soy soldado de Pancho Villa,
de sus dorados soy el mas fiel;
nada me importa perder la vida
si es cosa importa morir por el.

Ya llego, ya esta aqui,
Pancho Villa con su gente;
con sus dorados valientes
que por el han de morir.

I am a soldier of Pancho Villa,
of his dorados I am most faithful;
it matters not to me to lose my life,
if it is important to die for him.

He is come, he is here,
Pancho Villa and his people;
with his brave dorados
that for him may have to die.

During her performance a man stood up and walked out. He later
returned, apologized to her, and explained, "I have never been able
to hear that song because my father was killed by the Villistas. But I
understand now that Villa was considered a hero by many people."

On her trip home Jenny stopped at the Local 890 union hall
in Bayard, where she performed a Mexican folk ballad called
"El Deportado," (not to be confused with Woody Guthrie's
"Deportees") which she had discovered in a Texas Folklore Society
publication. In the front row, an elderly woman sang along.

Los gueros son muy maloras
Los gueros son muy maloras
Se valen de la occasion
Y a todos lo mexicanos
Y a todos los mexicanos
Los tratan sin compasion.

The white-skinned men are very wicked
The white-skinned men are very wicked
They take advantage of the occasion
And all the Mexicans
And all the Mexicans
Are treated without compassion.

The next day the same woman brought Jenny a book of Mexican songs, apologizing for its tattered condition. Jenny was deeply moved by the gift, which is still in her possession. That same day Jenny took her accordion to the picket line where she led the striking women in rousing renditions of "Solidarity Forever," "We Shall Not Be Moved," and "Union Maid."

In January 1952, after fifteen months, Empire Zinc and Local 890 reached an agreement. The union won most of its demands. With the conclusion of the strike, union men who at first had resisted the involvement of women, who had felt their very manhood threatened, now acknowledged the sacrifices the women made and the risks they had taken. Women had revitalized the union and ensured the successful outcome of the strike. They had proven themselves a force no longer to be denied.

Immediately following the settlement, however, twenty union men and women were charged with contempt of court. The defendants were determined to go to jail rather than pay fines to Empire Zinc. When the news of the charges was announced, Jenny and Craig, and their neighbors Carlos Trujillo and Juan Arellano, put their properties on the line to raise a bond of more than $27,000 to keep the accused out of jail. Craig issued a statement: "We feel that the Empire Zinc Company not only failed to provide wages and conditions of employment equal to the standards established by other mines in the Silver City area but this company, owned by eastern capital, and found guilty by the National Labor Relations Board of unfair labor practices, also provoked the violence which marked the strike."

Columnist James Barber responded in the *Raton Daily Range*, "What goes on at this San Cristobal ranch north of Taos?" Barber then rehashed some of the accusations commonly levied against Craig and Jenny—that the Progressive Party had been a captive of the Communist Party and that the ranch catered to communists. "Voters may want to examine some of those things before they cast their ballots in the Democratic primary election in May. Vincent is seeking nomination in Taos County as Democratic candidate for state representative." (It was Craig's one and only run for public office in New Mexico. He was not nominated.)

Neither the Jenckses nor the Vincents could have been surprised by the unrelenting interest the FBI was taking in them. One of Clint's visits to the ranch in 1950 coincided with the week that Harvey Matusow was in residence. Now, in 1952, Matusow delivered his first public testimony before the House Committee on Un-American Activities (HUAC) and he pointed the finger at San Cristobal Valley Ranch.

With his HUAC and subsequent Senate Internal Security Subcommittee (SISS) testimony, Matusow achieved what he had wanted all along, which was the same thing McCarthy wanted—to be page-one news. The attacks so irritated Taos resident Mariana Howes that she wrote to *El Crepusculo*, Taos's weekly newspaper. "So the pointing finger of one Harvey M. Matusow, testifying before the House Un-American Activities Committee, has singled out for suspicion one of our most beloved citizens, Jennie Wells Vincent, and her husband Craig. And, in doing so, has made front-page headlines in *El Crepusculo*. That is snappy journalism. We all know Jennie and love her gay folk-singing which has always added so much to our fiestas in Taos. . . . Such menacingly suspicious reports really belong in the 'How Silly Can You Be?' department."

Jenny and Craig could chuckle over Matusow's wild accusation that ranch guests had gone on an intelligence-gathering expedition to Los Alamos. (It was an excursion to Bandelier National Monument, an archaeological site.) "The truth is we are interested in atomic energy," Craig and Jenny retorted in a published statement. "We want the atomic bomb outlawed by all nations. We want atomic energy used in every peacetime way that scientists can devise to lighten the work and improve the health and welfare of all people." But they did not laugh when they learned that the FBI had tried to enlist some of their neighbors to keep track of the names and license plate numbers of ranch guests. They did not laugh when Archbishop Byrne of Santa Fe threatened excommunication for anyone who continued to affiliate with people from the ranch. As Jenny recalls, the following weekend's community night at the ranch drew the largest attendance ever.

On a subsequent visit to Jenny's ranch, Clint Jencks met film producer Paul Jarrico and told him about the Mine Mill strike. Intrigued by the story and the image of women on the picket line, Jarrico contacted his brother-in-law, screenwriter Michael Wilson, and director Herbert Biberman. The three men, who were blacklisted in Hollywood (all had been members of the Communist Party since its heyday during the Depression), had recently formed Independent Productions Corporation to make "real films about real working people," the kind of movies on which Hollywood was turning its back. Jencks's story seemed perfect. It would be called *Salt of the Earth*, and in an inspired move the filmmakers decided to use many of the actual strikers in the movie. The few outsiders in the film included Mexican star Rosaura Revueltas as the female lead opposite union leader Juan Chacon, Will Geer as the sheriff, and Clinton and Virginia Jencks essentially playing themselves.

Filming began on January 20, 1953. On February 9 the *Hollywood Reporter* said, "H'wood Reds are shooting a feature length anti-American racial issue propaganda movie at Silver City, N.M." Threats to and attacks on the crew soon followed. Ten days before the film wrapped, Revueltas was arrested and deported to Mexico on the grounds that her passport was invalid. Craig, who regularly visited the New Mexico State Legislature in Santa Fe to stay apprised of political events, encouraged Gov. Ed Meacham to mobilize the National Guard to protect the filmmakers. The final days of filming were completed under the protection of the New Mexico State Police. Nevertheless, on March 7, when filming ended, two union halls and the home of a union leader were set afire.

Once it was finished, the film came under further assault from politicians who did not want it on the nation's screens. California Congressman Donald Jackson cabled millionaire Howard Hughes, who responded with a lesson in how to sabotage a movie's release by intimidating lab technicians, musicians, editors, and others whose postproduction services are indispensable to a movie's release. Laboratories and technicians were threatened with the blacklist, but a young cameraman named Haskell Wexler secretly processed the film in Chicago. Over the years *Salt of the Earth* has gained cult status as a groundbreaking film for its prolabor stance, focus on Mexican Americans, use of actual strikers in the film, and outspoken feminism.

Perhaps coincidentally, four days before *Salt of the Earth* started filming, the McCarran Committee (SISS) requested from the FBI "a summary of any derogatory information" the bureau had about Jenny and Craig. There was plenty. For the past few years informants had been reporting on their every move. Some of the documentation borders on the comic. Back in May 1950, for example, Jenny led guests in singing the traditional African American spiritual "Oh, Freedom" ("And before I'll be a slave / I'll be buried in my grave / and go home to my Lord"). An informant described the song as having "a definite Communist tinge." Later that year: "Confidential informant (name deleted) of known reliability" reported on meetings at the ranch during which "racial propaganda, peace, and other Communist propaganda" had been presented. There was even someone at the ranch the day Harvey Matusow appeared who informed on the arrival of the informer. But most reports were in deadly earnest. Names of guests were recorded and circulated to FBI field offices around the country. Specimens of Jenny's handwriting found their way into FBI labs.

In November 1953 the *Rocky Mountain News* published an article with the headline "Ex-Denverite Hedges at Red Tie-Up Probe." The story announced that the SISS had made public testimony that Craig had given in June, saying that Craig refused on the grounds that he might incriminate himself to answer questions as to whether he was then a member of the Communist Party and whether the ranch was operating as an adjunct of the party.

Clinton Jencks went on trial in January 1954 in El Paso, accused of falsely signing a Taft-Hartley affidavit that he was not a communist. Subpoenaed to testify, Craig refused to produce a guest register from the ranch. It was news all over the West. *The Denver Post* even printed some headlines in red. Craig "stood on his constitutional rights, invoking the Fifth Amendment in refusing to answer any questions as to his ownership or operation of the ranch or the existence of a guest register," The *El Paso Times* reported. Later that month the *Albuquerque Journal* reported that Craig's sentencing had been delayed; finally, in March, the charges were dropped. Jencks did not fare as well. The jury deliberated only twenty-two minutes before finding him guilty and sentencing him to five years in prison.

From April 22 to June 17, 1954, millions of Americans watched the bizarre and disorderly Army-McCarthy hearings unfold on television. Joe McCarthy's accusations that the army had failed to root out communists from its ranks proved his undoing. He was censured by the Senate later that year, and in 1957 died of acute alcoholism. By the time of the Army-McCarthy hearings, Harvey Matusow's personal and professional lives had unraveled, and he began to recant much of his previous testimonies. In 1955 he published his story in a book entitled *False Witness*. While it was being printed he signed two affidavits, in one of which he recanted his testimony against Clinton Jencks.

The book caused a sensation. Matusow appeared once more before the SISS, this time to swear that the contents of the book were true and that the overwhelming percentage of his previous testimonies was false. Matusow was indicted for scheming to obstruct justice and spent three-and-a-half years in prison. In April 1955 John Steinbeck wrote in the *Saturday Review*, "I suspect that government informers, even if they had told the truth, can't survive Matusow's testimony. He has said that it was a good racket. It will never be so good again." Steinbeck was right. The Justice Department shut down its paid informants program. After

Matusow's recantation, Jencks wrote him a letter "welcoming him back to the human race. He was obviously an oddball, and his great ability was as a liar. He could take a perfectly innocent encounter and make up the rest."

That same year Jenny and Craig, along with Albert Kahn, who had published *False Witness*, were called before a grand jury in New York to face possible charges that they were part of a conspiracy that had paid Matusow to recant. Coincidentally, Jenny was scheduled to perform in New York for a Latin American cultural organization; to great applause she sang the same Pancho Villa ballad she had sung to the Salt of the Earth strikers. At the hearing Craig produced a photocopy of a check that the *Santa Fe New Mexican* had paid to Matusow for an article which he had, in fact, plagiarized from *Political Affairs* magazine. The charges were dismissed. Clinton Jencks, however, had to wait until 1957 for the U.S. Supreme Court to overturn his conviction.

The era of the paid informer was over, but for Jenny and Craig the damage Matusow and others had done was irreparable. In 1953, two years before *False Witness*, they had sold their ranch. In a letter to the Taos Chamber of Commerce, Craig explained: "For two years now we have been the target of ceaseless attack, growing out of the fabrication of a single person who has kept embellishing his story to suit his needs. Under the cloak of Congressional immunity his accusations against us and others have been hashed and rehashed by Congressional committees and big city newspapers to ruin our reputation and business in the headlines. We decided that we could no longer in all fairness to our guests and ourselves subject them to the overt danger of being framed in this way, to satisfy the evil political purposes of those who would subvert the Constitution."

When Jenny sold her ranch a reporter from the *Albuquerque Journal* came to interview them. Craig agreed on one condition. He would give a statement if the newspaper printed it as he said it. "If it's any consolation to the Senate Internal Security Subcommittee," he said, "we've bought a small house and now live two miles closer to Los Alamos." ("And they printed it!" says Jenny. "Everybody got a kick out of that.") She and Craig had purchased an old two-room adobe house on seventeen acres down the valley from the ranch. The kitchen was in good shape and there was electricity, but the house had no running water and the ceiling in the second room was caving in.

For a month Jenny and Craig stayed in the home of Carlos and Pablita Trujillo, while the Trujillos temporarily moved up to the ranch, where they were going to work for the new owners. Their son, Jose Leon, stayed with the Vincents. Jenny and Craig even talked to the Trujillos about adopting Larry should anything happen to them. Craig worked on the house with help from neighbors, including Cleofes and Frances Vigil. As a teenager, Cleofes had worked for Jenny and Dan. Piano, desk, and bed went into one room; orange crates lined the walls for shelving. The second room was for Larry. The Vincents moved in July 1954 and immediately set about adding a second bedroom, bathroom, and a large music room. The FBI promptly added the Vincents' new house to its Master Search Warrant.

Jenny had gone to great lengths to make the ranch a part of the community. She had employed many local people, and now those jobs were gone. The guest ranch had operated for only four years. San Cristobal Valley Ranch had been solidly left-leaning to be sure, a refuge for like-minded individuals who could enjoy a brief respite from the swirling hysteria outside. It had also been a center for social activities, lectures, discussion groups, movies, athletic and outdoor events, art, theater, and, of course, music.

A generation of those who visited the ranch is gone, but sons and daughters of that generation retain vivid memories of it and its hostess. Linda Gordon came to the ranch as a child of ten with her mother and father and returned for a summer on her own. The Gordons lived in Denver, where Bill was a social worker and Helen a nursery school teacher. ("We were very, very non-wealthy," says Gordon, now an award-winning historian at New York University.)

Bill was part of a citizen's group that supported Mine Mill. One summer Jenny took Linda on as a "scholarship" student at the ranch. Linda had regular chores she was expected to perform, but had such a good time that she sometimes forgot them. She was too busy following around after a couple of young ranch hands whom all the girls were crazy about.

"Craig Vincent was charismatic," she recalls, "and Jenny extremely warm. There were counselors for the kids, but Jenny was always interacting with us. It was a working ranch with farming, gardening, and animals. What I didn't see then that I do now is how extraordinary it was that this Anglo couple was so completely dug in with the Spanish-speaking people around them."

Kim Chernin remembers Linda Gordon. A best-selling author, Chernin spent the summers of 1949 to 1951 at the ranch. Her parents, Paul Kusnitz and Rose Chernin Kusnitz, were communists. (In 1951, her mother was arrested in Los Angeles and sentenced to six months in jail.) "The ranch served as a haven for those on the left," Chernin says. "I remember Clinton Jencks there, speaking about the Salt of the Earth strike. I remember Jenny singing with Earl Robinson. Music and singing were integral components of the ranch culture, and Jenny was at the center of them. There were arts and crafts, a lot of horseback riding and hiking, and trips to the Taos Pueblo. I have a very strong sense of children being included in all the activities. Jenny always saw to that. Anywhere else we were outsiders, reluctant to be known, but there at that ranch we had a sense of belonging."

Chernin also remembers Earl Robinson's young nephew. During his two summers at the ranch, Alan Arkin did a little bit of everything. "I washed dishes, I was a busboy, I even cleaned the toilets," he recalls. The future film star was also a regular performer at ranch hootenannies and community nights, when he joined his uncle, Jenny, and such visiting folk singers as Walt Conley and Ernie Lieberman. Arkin was at the ranch the week Harvey Matusow showed up but doesn't remember him. He does remember such guests as blacklisted actor Howard Da Silva and singer Ronnie Gilbert of the Weavers. "Those two summers were the happiest times of my youth," Arkin says. "I attribute it to a wonderful feeling of fellowship there. Jenny was such a positive force, such a delightful person. I remember her singing, and I remember her commitment to making the ranch and San Cristobal all one community. Most of all, I just remember her shining presence."

EIGHT

Trio de Taos

The loss of her beloved ranch was a severe blow to Jenny, who had given so much of herself to it since 1937. But 1953 held a greater loss for her: on September 16 her mother died in Prairie View, Illinois. Deborah Sayles Hill Ferry was seventy-two. Her ashes were placed in Lake Forest Cemetery beside those of Frank Ferry and Abby Farwell Ferry. The memorial service in Evanston became a Ferry-Hill family reunion, as all of Jenny's surviving siblings and their spouses were in attendance. In two months, details of Deborah Ferry's will were recorded in Jenny's FBI file.

In the final years of Deborah Ferry's life, she and Jenny had remained close. Of course Jenny had made a conscious decision to live in circumstances that were quite different from those in which she had been raised, but that choice mirrored the independence Deborah herself had demonstrated many years earlier when she married Fred Hill. Living circumstances aside, Deborah had remained a strong role model for Jenny. "Personally, she came to mean even more to me after I remarried," Jenny says. "She was so pleased that I was now happy. She had been born into affluence, and in turn she always did so much for her children and for any community she lived in. She went to great lengths to teach us the virtue of gratitude. She always insisted that we express thanks to anyone for anything they may do for us. Frank Jr. and I have talked about this often, and to this day we remain appreciative for these good qualities that Mother taught us. She didn't believe in teaching manners for their own sake; teach thoughtfulness and the manners will follow."

Despite the personal losses and political turmoil of recent years, Jenny never considered leaving San Cristobal. She had been in the village for almost twenty years, a length of time that paled in comparison to the families that had lived there for generations, but sufficient nonetheless for Jenny to know that her first instincts about the village and its people had been correct. This was home. Her embrace of San Cristobal was consistent with the comfort she had experienced growing up in the two small communities of her family and North Shore Country Day School.

For Jenny, nobility has nothing to do with riches or royalty; nobility is reserved for the people who are salt of the earth, people who live more simple lives close to the ground and in communities. She never felt ostracized by the predominantly Catholic faith of her neighbors, for while Jenny is not religious in terms of affiliation with a single faith, she has always been spiritual. Growing up, she attended twelve years of Sunday school with forward-thinking teachers who discussed all religions. At North Shore, she participated in a group that brought representatives of different faiths in to speak. In spiritual matters, Jenny is ecumenical, not exclusionary.

In October and November Jenny and Craig visited his brother Bill at his farm in Port Townsend, Washington. By Thanksgiving Day a detailed report had been placed in Jenny's FBI file, including a six-page list of mail received at the farm (addressee, return address, postmark) and a two-page list of toll-call charges to the farm (date, number called, length of time, identity of caller).

That fall Jenny and Craig also visited Craig's old high school acquaintance, Dalton Trumbo, and his wife, Cleo, in California. Still blacklisted, Trumbo had nevertheless moved his family back to the United States after a period in Mexico City. Jenny recalls that while they were there a knock came on the door, and someone delivered a plain manila envelope to Dalton. "He told us that is how he receives everything, so it does not come through the mail."

While in the Los Angeles area Jenny performed on several occasions. "No indication of communist activity while in Los Angeles," read the FBI report. That tone changed slightly when Jenny flew to San Francisco, where she performed in a series of folk song recitals to benefit the California Labor School, the Northern California Peace Council, and the Independent Progressive Party. The labor school was one of many such institutions supported by labor unions and offering classes in everything from labor relations to line drawing. A leaflet announced three separate appearances by Jenny: on November 14, "Songs of all Nations"; on November 20, "Songs of Mexico and the Southwest"; and on November 21, "Indian, Mexican, and Latin American Folk Songs."

In 1952 Jenny had received a call from one Sarah Gertrude Knott. A native of Princeton, Kentucky, Knott founded the National Folk Festival in 1934 as one way to help raise national morale during the Depression. In her own way Sarah Knott was a visionary. Her enduring innovation was to stage the arts of many nations, races, and languages at the same event and with equal billing. W. C. Handy made his first performance on a desegregated stage at the 1938 festival, which Eleanor Roosevelt had helped bring to Washington, D.C. Zora Neale Hurston brought blues and black shape-note singers from Florida. (Among those who joined her as field workers or presenters were the writer J. Frank Dobie and the song collector and musician Bascomb Lamar Lunsford.) Sarah Knott envisioned the festival as a forum not for professional musicians and entertainers, although such acknowledged stars as Pete Seeger did participate, but for amateur folk musicians, dancers, and craftspeople. She was in the Southwest scouting regional talent when she contacted Jenny.

Sarah invited Jenny to perform first at a smaller festival in Albuquerque and after hearing her invited to perform at the national festival. It was the beginning of a long association with the festival and a personal friendship between director and performer. Jenny became an unofficial right-hand aide to Sarah, offering suggestions, conferring on festival details, and performing regularly. A lot of her performance effort went into the festival where, in addition to her own presentations, she would be on hand to play the piano for any groups or other acts that required backup. One of Jenny's festival favorites was Jimmy Driftwood (James Morris), a musician, folklorist, and teacher from Arkansas. Jimmy is best-known for writing "The Battle of New Orleans," made famous by Johnny Horton, which he wrote to help explain the War of 1812 to his high school history students, and "The Tennessee Stud," popularized by everyone from Eddy Arnold to Johnny Cash. At the 1955 festival Jenny sang with Jimmy and ballad singer May Kennedy McCord, the "First Lady of the Ozarks."

That same year Jenny returned to the California Labor School to perform with Pete Seeger. There she met W. E. B. DuBois and ran into her former Vassar classmate Muriel Rukeyser. Rukeyser was surprised to see Jenny—"She remembered me as that conservative piano player from college." Several days later Jenny joined Seeger in concert at a San Francisco union hall. Several years later Jenny would reunite with Seeger and Malvina Reynolds for a concert in Berkeley. "Malvina and her husband had been guests at the ranch, and she wrote a very nice song about San Cristobal," says Jenny. "She had a real gift for putting socially significant words to music." Seeger also gave concerts in New Mexico on two occasions during this time, once staying at Jenny's house.

The national folk festivals provided Jenny with widespread exposure, but perhaps the most important development in her music at that time took place back home. Jenny had heard about a local mandolin player, so one day in 1956 she went to hear her at the Mabel Dodge Luhan House. Jenny introduced herself and right away the mandolinist wanted to know if they could get together and play.

This was Hattie Trujillo. Born Hattie Marsten on Staten Island, New York, Hattie received her first mandolin from her mother and began studying when she was very young. After her mother's death, Hattie moved to Albuquerque to live with a relative. She met Ed Trujillo, from a politically well-appointed Taos family, and married him in 1925. The Trujillos lived in Taos and raised their three children there (a historical marker is on their house today).

Jenny and Hattie began as a duo called Las Palomas (the Doves). Soon, Hattie introduced Jenny to Nat Flores, a guitarist with whom Hattie had previously played. Originally from Deming, New Mexico, Nat moved with his family to Taos when he was quite young. He married Claudine Montoya, whose brother was with the seminal New Mexican musical group Los Alegres (the Happy Ones). One of Nat's important early gigs was with a dance band that regularly played Mike Cunico's nightclub in Taos. In the 1930s Jenny had danced there with Frieda, Angelino, and Dan. Before long Jenny, Hattie, and Nat formed the Trio de Taos; they debuted on KOA radio in Denver as part of "A Salute to Taos," a program organized by Ruth Fish.

The Trio de Taos would become one of New Mexico's most popular musical groups and would perform together without personnel change for thirty years, an almost unheard-of length of time for any musical ensemble. Critical to the trio's success was that it performed an eclectic repertoire—a check of set lists over the years reveals everything from songs of the WPA archives to "Hello, Dolly," "Ramblin' Rose," and "Blue Eyes Cryin' in the Rain"— and that it played for dancing. All three musicians had experience playing Dixieland, swing, jitterbug, and everything in between for dances. While any number of indigenous musicians played traditional folk songs of the area, they did so in an idiosyncratic manner. Folklorist, musician, and writer Jack Loeffler referred to this music as *musica de los viejitos*, after a quip by local musician Vicente Montoya. As Loeffler has written, "One characteristic of folk music is that it is passed from musician to musician through oral tradition.... Since folk music notation, whether vocal or instrumental, is rarely written down, each performance is subject to varying degrees of recollection, technical expertise, interpretation, and style. No piece is performed exactly the same way twice." Jenny recognized this as one of the distinctive charms of folk music, yet while she and Hattie could improvise while playing, the Trio de Taos became renowned for its reliable dance beat.

"If you play for dancing you have to play in measurable time," Jenny says. "People often told us that our music didn't sound exactly like that of the other groups who played these songs, and that is why: We structured the music with exact rhythm, we counted the measures. Most of the musicians here play by ear and of course, with my background, I appreciate that. Their phrasing is individualistic, which is wonderful but can be difficult to accompany or to dance to. For dancing, you can't lose the beat."

From Tin Pan Alley pop ("Five Foot Two, Eyes of Blue") to western swing ("San Antonio Rose"), traditional Spanish-American dances even to rock and roll ("But we couldn't master 'the Twist'"), the trio had a ball. Hattie routinely carried the thickest briefcase Jenny had ever seen, stuffed with her music. Jenny told her she didn't need it as all the music was in her head, but the briefcase was her security blanket. Unlike Jenny and Hattie, Nat couldn't read music, but he had honed an impeccable sense of rhythm and laid down a driving foundation for Hattie's mandolin and Jenny's accordion and vocals.

Not only did Jenny now have the Trio de Taos, she launched her own record label, Cantemos Records, and opened Taos's only music store. In 1956 she released her first solo recording, *Spanish-American Children's Songs: Folksongs for Children of All Ages*. The album features ten songs from Mexico, South America, Spain, and the southwestern U.S., which Jenny sang in English and Spanish to her own guitar or accordion accompaniment (she had taught herself the rudiments of folk guitar since living in New Mexico). The record proved extremely popular and even today remains in use in schools. With it Jenny provided a bilingual lyric sheet with guitar chords and comments on the provenance of each song.

Jenny followed the children's recording with *Spanish Folksongs of the Americas*, another set of ten bilingual songs from throughout the Americas that she sang to her guitar and accordion. As with the children's record, Jenny provided notes on the origin of each song, adhering to her conviction that credit should be given where credit is due. She sent a copy to Paul Robeson. After accompanying the singer during the Wallace campaign, Jenny was never to see Robeson again, only speak with him on the phone. At his farewell New York concert in Carnegie Hall, Robeson sang a lullaby from the record, explaining that he learned it from Jenny Vincent in San Cristobal, New Mexico.

To the people of Taos County, the page-one announcement began:

> Here we are up to our necks in printer's ink. Because a
> statement of policy is expected by every new publisher,
> here is ours. *El Crepusculo* is a community newspaper.
> It is owned, edited, written, made up and printed by
> people who live in Taos. This newspaper is responsible
> to the people of Taos County—all of the people. We who
> work on the paper shall be devoted to our duty to all of
> the people in our county. You who read it and advertise
> in it have a right and a duty to criticize or approve of
> our efforts. This newspaper is not tied to any group,
> special interest, or political party. It is an independent,
> hometown paper. We shall print the news objectively.
> When you believe we have not been fair, let us know.
> We want to work for those things which will help our
> community. Those differences which now exist should
> and can be solved in a friendly and democratic fashion on
> the basis of what is right for the community as a whole.

The statement was signed and dated July 30, 1959, by the paper's new publisher, Craig Vincent. Craig had leased the paper from Edward Cabot for one year with an option to buy it. His inaugural issue demonstrated that in addition to the births, marriages, obituaries, local sports, and other staples of hometown papers, there would be political news and reports on corporate shenanigans. The traditional "Seccion Espanol" would continue, and regular columns included "'Dobe Dust" by Ruth Fish and "Sage & Cacatus" [sic] by doughBelly Price. The premier issue featured a report on the Fiesta de Taos, including music by Los Charros, Las Palomas, and children in Ruth Rael's class at the Fish Hatchery School "singing Spanish folk songs and dancing children's dances from Germany." Rael's students were photographed with an accompanying accordionist, the likely source of their German numbers. "Jenny's gift of giving and helping is and will always be a fond memory for the students, parents, and teachers of the Fish Hatchery," Rael later said.

Craig soon brought in John Collier to write on Indian culture. In the 1920s Congress had considered a bill that would hand over Indian land and water rights without compensation to developers. That bill failed but a replacement soon appeared, and Collier crusaded against it. The campaign attracted many artists and writers. Even D. H. Lawrence got into the act, penning an article for the *New York Times* and joining Carl Sandburg, Zane Grey, Vachel Lindsay, and Edgar Lee Masters to sign a petition of protest. Collier would go on to become a highly respected author and U.S. Commissioner of Indian Affairs.

It wasn't long before Craig felt compelled to place an editorial on page one. "This paper has no affiliation or connection with any political party—Republican, Democrat, Socialist, Prohibitionist or (we should not have to point out) Communist. Since last week's attack singled out the publisher of this paper, let us remind our readers that Craig Vincent is not a Communist: he has been a member of the Democratic Party since 1931. . . . Once again, *El Crepusculo* is an independent newspaper, serving no special interests whatsoever."

Craig was telling the truth. In 1956 Soviet Premier Nikita Khrushchev revealed what many around the world had previously only suspected: the reign of his predecessor Joseph Stalin had been one of incalculable crimes against his own people. Within weeks thousands abandoned the Communist Party in America, ending whatever effect it may have had. In a year it was reduced to what it had once been, a small marginal sect. By the time Craig penned his editorial in November 1959, he and Jenny had long since left the party.

In that same issue Craig published a photograph of *El Crepusculo*'s staff, which included editor Edward Abbey, Spanish section editor Felix Valdes, art director Rini Templeton, photographer Mildred Crews, printer Judson Crews, and columnists Fish, Price, Otto Pitcher, and Sra. Jesusita Perrault. The photo is evidence of Craig's ability to attract an exceptional group of people. Templeton was on the cusp of becoming renowned for both her activism and her art, which she regularly gave away to political causes. Judson Crews was already a widely known avant-garde poet and small press publisher and his wife, Mildred, an outstanding photographer. The following year Abbey would publish *The Brave Cowboy*, the basis for the 1962 Kirk Douglas film *Lonely Are the Brave* (with a script by Dalton Trumbo), and be on his way to *Desert Solitaire* and *The Monkey Wrench Gang*.

In January 1960 Craig's support of Spanish Civil War refugees brought angry letters. "I shall appreciate your sparing us any further public manifestation of your prejudices," wrote Rev. Gerard Litjens of Questa, "when they carry any manifestation of sympathy with a communist group or cause, in this our *El Crepusculo*, with its fair traditions of the past, and of which I am still a subscriber in spite of the grave crisis through which it has passed and from which it is still suffering." Abbey retorted that to call all Spanish Republican refugees communists fighting for communism is like accusing anyone who opposed Franco of being pro-Stalin. Equating antifascism with procommunism, he said, is an affront to good men everywhere.

Abbey's tenure on the newspaper was brief and tumultuous, lasting only from October 1959 through January 1960. He had been living in Albuquerque when Craig approached him. Against his iconoclastic instincts, Abbey decided to give the job a go, but he found it so time-consuming that he couldn't write anything else. He also chafed under authority, regardless of how loosely it was applied. Where Craig was serious and political, Abbey was sardonic and anarchistic. "It's hard to say if he quit or was fired," says Judson Crews, "but it was probably mutual." Abbey was happy to leave behind both journalism and what he called the hip-boutique city of Taos. "Ed was a wonderful guy, but a real character," says Mildred Crews (now Mildred Tolbert). "And Craig was a complex man himself. To Judson and I it seemed inevitable that they would clash." Nevertheless a few years later the tensions had eased sufficiently for Abbey to take Craig and Jenny on a summer boat trip.

Mildred and Judson had met in Taos in 1947 and on their first date heard Jenny perform at the Blue Door Gallery. In addition to being a prolific poet, Judson was a job printer who worked out of the newspaper's back shop. He considered the paper overstaffed. "It was a big staff that groaned and grunted until late at night many nights of the week to get the paper out," he says. "I personally liked Craig. He obviously ruffled some local feathers, but I never found him particularly argumentative. But he was not a real business-man." After the Litjens-Abbey exchange, Craig would publish only three more issues of *El Crepusculo*. Pressed by competition—the *Santa Fe New Mexican* had launched the weekly *Taos News*—and continually confronted with accusations about his political affiliations, Craig could only stand by and watch as advertisers withdrew from the paper; *El Crepusculo* suffered the same fate as San Cristobal Valley Ranch.

Jenny, Larry, and Craig Vincent,
Denver, 1948.

Joe Santistevan, Progressive Party presidential
candidate Henry Wallace, Pete Tagger:
San Cristobal Valley Ranch, summer 1948.

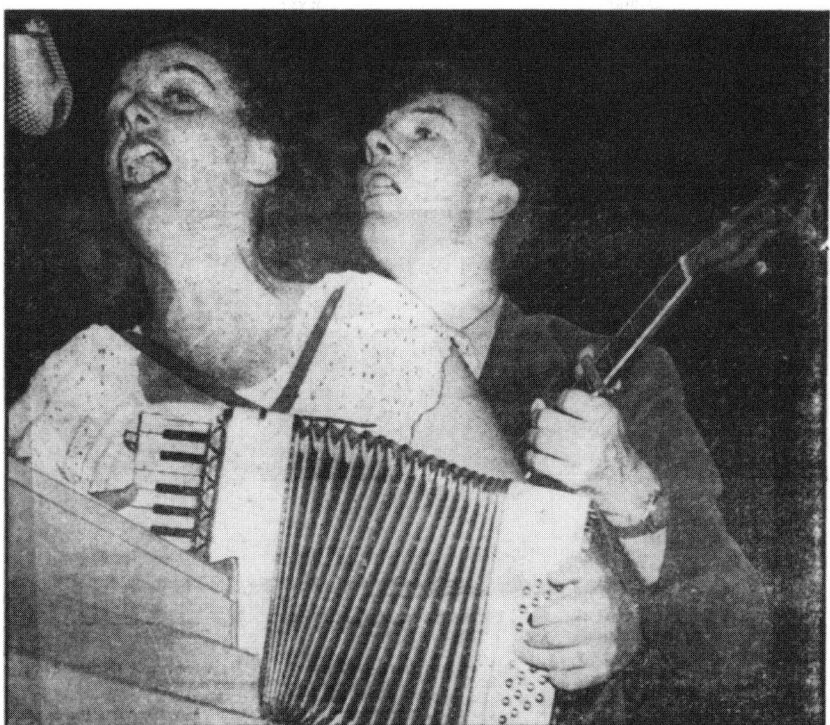

Two People's Songsters at the mike at the Progressive Party Convention.

**The Progressive Party added many new things to America...
one is the rebirth of a people's culture, songs of the people**

News clipping of Jenny performing with
Pete Seeger at Progressive Party presidential
nominating convention, Philadelphia, July 1948.

Jenny performing at an annual convention
of the International Union of Mine,
Mill and Smelters Workers.

Singer, actor, activist Paul Robeson, left,
and composer Earl Robinson in an undated
photograph. Jenny once accompanied Robeson,
one of her idols, during the 1948 Progressive
Party presidential campaign. Robinson ("Joe
Hill," "The House I Live In") was a frequent
visitor to Jenny's San Cristobal ranch. Photo
courtesy of University of Washington Libraries,
Special Collections UW17917.

Jenny on the patio of San
Cristobal Valley Ranch, 1949.

Esperanza's saint's day celebration.
Publicity still, *Salt of the Earth*, ca. 1954.
Those pictured include, from left, Clinton
Jencks, with bottle, Henrietta Williams, with
bottle, Rosaura Revueltas, holding child,
and Juan Chacon, behind Revueltas. Photo
courtesy of Western Federation of Miners and
International Union of Mine, Mill and Smelter
Workers Collection, Archives, University of
Colorado at Boulder Libraries.

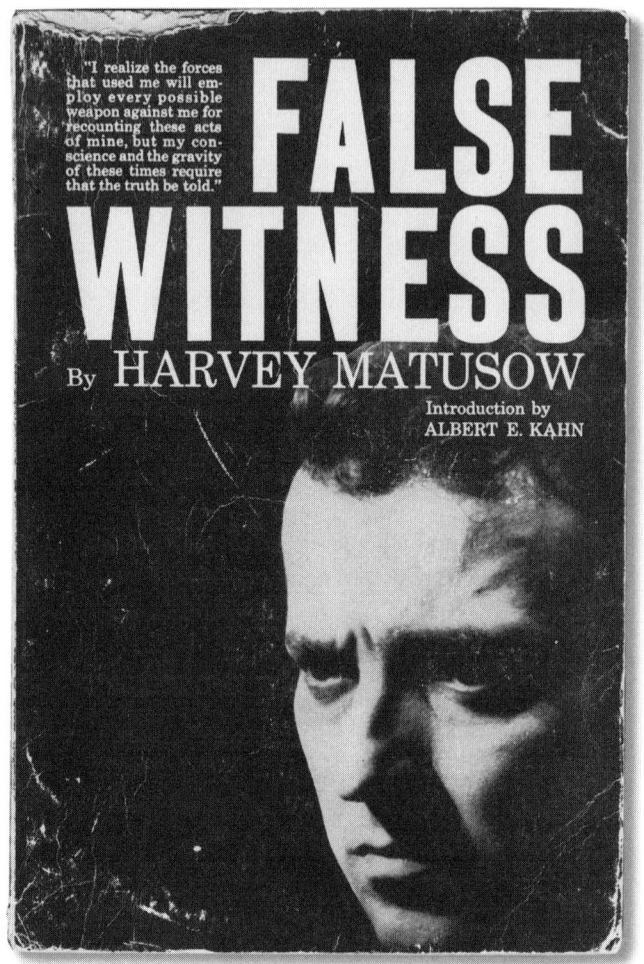

Book cover of *False Witness*
by FBI informant Harvey
Matusow, 1955.

LEFT:
Jenny performing with Pete Concha of Taos Pueblo at Hondo Lodge, Taos Ski Valley, 1960s.

BELOW:
Jenny performing for schoolchildren on San Juan Pueblo in the 1960s. Mildred Tolbert photo.

The Trio de Taos performing at the
Fiesta de Taos in the 1970s:
Nat Flores, Hattie Trujillo, Jenny.

Craig Vincent in the 1970s.
John Nichols photo.

The Jenny Vincent Trio: Rick Klein,
Jenny, Audrey Davis. Bill Davis photo.

In September 2006 Amy Goodman of radio's
"Democracy Now" spoke in Taos at a benefit for
Cultural Energy, which was launching a nonprofit,
educational radio station for northern New Mexico.
During the event the Jenny Vincent Trio performed,
and Goodman recorded Jenny singing her own
"God Bless the Americas." Pictured behind are
Audrey Davis and Rick Klein. Robin Collier photo,
courtesy of Cultural Energy.

Jenny Vincent outside her home in
San Cristobal, New Mexico, 2006.
Photograph by Dorie Hagler.

NINE

Are You Now or Have You Ever Been?

On 1960 Jenny and a friend, Joan Reno, founded Taos Recordings and Publications as a complement to her Cantemos Records. Whereas she would continue to issue her own recordings on the Cantemos label, with TRP Jenny wanted to preserve and promote other northern New Mexico music and musicians. She had been the beneficiary of the region's rich folk traditions since arriving in the 1930s, and now she wanted to give something back. Jenny envisioned TRP as a nonprofit organization. (It would remain that way: "Our expenses ran way over any income.") She also organized a volunteer board of directors that represented Taos's three cultures—indigenous tribal peoples, Latinos, and Anglos—and which included at various times Grace Collier, Isabel Concha, Mildred Crews, Guadalupe Vaughn, and Frances Vigil, as well as Joan and herself.

For TRP's first release she set up a reel-to-reel tape recorder in the back of the Taos Music Center and recorded a set of songs by Pete Concha. The *cacique* or spiritual leader from Taos Pueblo sang secular songs for the record and accompanied himself on native drums. Concha had done similar songs when he and Jenny appeared together at a ski lodge in Taos Ski Valley.

The response was encouraging. A March 1962 piece in the *Albuquerque Review* praised Concha for his "special flair as a performer, and his rich tonal latitude of voice in his chants." Taos Recordings and Publications, the review concluded, "feels that there is a real need not only to preserve the wealth of songs, folktales, plays, dances, and chants of northern New Mexico but to offer them as a source of pleasure and enrichment for the reader." Taos Recordings and Publications would later issue a second record by Concha, including a lullaby performed by his wife, Isabel. TRP produced the recordings on seven-inch, 33-rpm LPs. In those days, says Jenny, we called them compact disks.

One evening in Taos Ski Valley, two women approached Jenny and asked her if she would sing for their folk music club in Los Alamos. As it turned out, her performance was held in the home of Lois Bradbury, whose husband, Norris, had succeeded J. Robert Oppenheimer as head of the Los Alamos Nuclear Laboratory. Jenny had already met Lois through their mutual membership in the American Orff-Schulwerk Association, which promoted the music teaching method of Carl Orff. Lois was director of music for elementary and middle schools in Los Alamos. Jenny would indeed sing in the Los Alamos schools as well as for a peace group composed largely of laboratory employees. "All the time I was being persecuted during the McCarthy period, my records were being used in Los Alamos."

In June 1960 Jenny was waiting to go on stage at the National Folk Festival in Washington, D.C., when she heard someone paging her name. I'm Jenny Vincent, she replied. This is for you, said a messenger, handing her an envelope. It was a subpoena to appear the very next day before the Senate Internal Security Subcommittee.

Jenny and Craig had come to Washington a few days earlier, and at Sarah Knott's request Jenny granted an interview to the *Washington Evening Star*. The reporter, as it turned out, was married to the daughter of a scientist at Los Alamos. He loved New Mexico and told Jenny she was lucky to live there. The story was published without a byline on May 31, the day before the festival was to begin, under the headline, "'Secret Weapon' Tuned for Start of Folk Festival Here Tomorrow."

Among the 1,000 performers pouring into Washington for the four-day folk festival that starts tomorrow is a woman from New Mexico who feels her music can do much more than entertain.

Like many a visitor from the land of atomic laboratories and missile ranges, Mrs. Vincent comes to Washington with a secret weapon which she'll bring right out in the spotlight when she performs Friday and Saturday at the Carter Barron Amphitheatre.

What makes her big Spanish guitar a secret weapon, Jenny feels, is that many don't realize how the music she makes with it, as well as all folk music, can create a better understanding of people.

Jenny came to Taos, an art colony a scant hour's drive north of the atomic research town of Los Alamos, twenty-two years ago. She had spent her girlhood in Northfield, Minnesota, where her father was a professor of bible at Carleton College, and four years at Vassar, where she majored in music.

In the little town named after an ancient and still thriving Indian pueblo, she found herself enveloped by Southwestern culture and fascinated by the music. She became the owner of Taos' only music shop.

Dismayed that the Spanish-speaking people were being urged to forget Spanish and learn English, she set to work learning the local songs both in English and Spanish. Since 1955 she has made four records—two

78s and two LPs—that have been welcomed by musical, educational, and children's publications and approved as education aids by several school systems.

The unfortunate attempt at humor in the headline and the mention of Los Alamos was all it took—that and the name Vincent, which was still fodder for FBI files. That night, conservative radio commentator Fulton Lewis Jr., a supporter of Joseph McCarthy, lambasted Jenny on his program, the text of which was largely reprinted in the following day's edition of his newsletter, *The Top of the News with Fulton Lewis, Jr.* After reprinting the *Evening Star* piece, Lewis continued:

> So Mrs. Jenny Wells Vincent gets herself a big write-up for the Folk Festival, with picture and all. Now let's see who she is.
>
> Mrs. Jeannette Wells Vincent, commonly known as Jenny Wells Vincent, has established quite a following in the so-called "progressive circles" throughout the Southwest and West for quite some time.
>
> The January 1952 issue of MARCH OF LABOR, an ultra liberal publication, carried a music number entitled "Viva La Mine and Mill." It was explained that Jenny Wells, the composer, had appeared as a folk singer at four consecutive conventions of the International Union of Mine, Mill and Smelter Workers and at the last convention at Nogales, Arizona, her song was adopted as the theme song of the convention.
>
> The Mine, Mill, and Smelter Workers Union is one of the most notorious unions on record and was expelled from the C.I.O. on February 15, 1950 on charges of communist domination.
>
> Peoples Artists Inc. published a song pamphlet during the early 1950s and Jenny Wells Vincent was one of the contributors therein with a song entitled "De Los Dorados de Pancho Villa." This song depicted

the bandit Pancho Villa as a hero who fought tyranny
and oppression. Peoples Artists, Inc. was cited by the
California State Committee on Un-American Activities
as a communist front organization.

During November 1954 and October 1955, Jenny
gave a series of folk singing concerts in San Francisco,
which were sponsored by the California Labor School,
an organization which has been listed as subversive and
communist on the Attorney General's lists and which was
described by the Senate Internal Security Subcommittee
as follows:

"Schools under patriotic and benevolent titles
indoctrinate communists and outsiders in the theory and
practice of communism, train organizers and operatives,
recruit new party members and sympathizers. Schools
of this type include the California Labor School of San
Francisco."

The *People's Daily World*, West Coast communist
publication, in its issue of October 27, 1955, carried a
feature article regarding Jenny Wells Vincent together
with her picture. This article, in addition to lauding
the facilities at Vincent's guest ranch, the San Cristobal
Valley Ranch near Taos, New Mexico, recommended
the purchase of folk song recordings by Vincent and
attendance at her forthcoming concert, sponsored by
the California Labor School.

The San Cristobal Ranch, when it was owned and
operated by Jenny and her husband, Craig Stephen
Vincent, was referred to by members of the Senate
Internal Security Subcommittee on May 28, 1953. At
this time Craig Vincent invoked the Fifth Amendment
approximately 26 times to questions concerning not
only his own Communist Party membership, but that
of his wife, including questions concerning the use
of the ranch by the Communist Party as a place of
indoctrination of communists.

So there she is, Jenny Wells Vincent, who shows up here is [*sic*] Washington as one of the performers in this national Folk Festival which begins tonight, with a guitar which she calls her secret weapon.

From newspaper to radio to newsletter, it was remarkably fast work. Seven years after losing their ranch to McCarthyism, all of the old suspicions about the subversive Vincents were raised again. Jenny's appearance before the subcommittee was delayed until after the conclusion of the festival. On June 2, James Ford of the National Capital Committee Board of Trade contacted the FBI wanting to know if the rumors about Jenny were true. He was told that FBI files were confidential, but he might check with the HUAC. Ford said he understood that Jenny had been subpoenaed by the SISS, and that he planned to prevent her from appearing at the festival. She was subsequently yanked from the festival and not permitted to perform.

Was this the chamber where the Army-McCarthy hearings had been televised a few years ago? Looking around, Jenny couldn't be sure; she was nervous nonetheless. It was June 6, 1960. As she waited for the hearing to begin, she watched senators, staff members, and people in the audience milling about in anticipation of the arrival of Chairman James O. Eastland, the segregationist senator from Mississippi. While she sat with lawyer David Rein (Craig was not permitted to be with her) and wondered if this hearing would result in her being indicted, Jenny wrote out music for Hattie. A member of the committee asked her what she was doing. When she explained, he smiled and told her he also played the mandolin. They chatted amiably for a few minutes, but when the hearing convened the smile vanished from his face, and he turned on his heel to take his seat. Eastland never did appear; another member of the committee conducted the hearing. When Jenny was called, she was prepared with a statement she and Craig had written.

I came to Washington to sing at the National Folk
Festival, as I have for the last seven years, to sing the
Spanish language and cowboy songs which are a part of
the folk culture in the Southwest, where I live.

Music has been a natural part of my life since early
childhood. It is my profession, my hobby, and my business.

Participation in the National Folk Festival means to me
a sharing of folk music, songs and dances, a sharing that
leads to better understanding among peoples. The director
of the National Folk Festival, Sarah Gertrude Knott, well
expresses my own views when she says, 'As long as our
people can come together in friendship and good will
to present the folk songs and dances of their choice or
inheritance, regardless of race, nationality, or creed, we can
rest assured that culture and freedom, now denied many
peoples of the world, are still our precious heritage.'

President Eisenhower echoes these thoughts when
he says of the National Folk Festival, 'It is a dramatic
reminder that our individual freedoms and national
strength come from the interplay of diverse social forces
directed toward a common goal.'

The National Folk Festival will best serve democracy
as long as it can freely present these diverse folk
traditions that are so important in creating friendship
among all peoples. It will cease to serve democracy the
minute it is required to screen its participants on the basis
of creed, whether it be social, religious, or political.

As for the Eastland Committee, I have no intention
to sing for it. I do not sing its theme song of bigotry. I
believe our country needs to breathe the full fresh air of
freedom, and we will be able to breathe better when this
committee, and its counterpart the House Un-American
Activities Committee, are abolished.

It was over in half an hour. Jenny remembers the questioning
as token and, surprisingly, without demands that she name names,

which she was fully prepared not to do. An entry in her FBI files claims she invoked the Fifth Amendment "approximately 119 times," which must be either a typographical error or a world record. Rein later told Craig that the nature of the committee's questions suggested that Fulton Lewis was cooperating with the committee and may even have inspired the issuance of the subpoena. "The issue is typical of the kind of broadcasts he has been making for about the last twenty years," Rein said. "He has recently been an unsuccessful defendant in several libel suits."

The day after the Lewis broadcast, Henry Cape, a director of Baltic Mills in which the Ferry/Sayles families had an interest, wrote to Baltic counsel Hayward Parsons. "You will remember my pretty frankly expressed feelings about 'Vincent' after the three-cornered chat you, he, and I had maybe a couple of years ago," Cape said. "I now feel pretty well justified!! Last night . . . Fulton Lewis Jr. . . . devoted considerable time to exposing Jennie Wells Vincent and her husband. He told of her playing and singing in Spanish and English and of her record shop where records she sells are inductive to communistic principles at times. Vincent has invoked the Fifth Amendment twenty-six times. . . . [They] it seemed also ran a motel or guest ranch which was used for recruiting commies."

Jenny's siblings received copies of Cape's diatribe, and Frank Jr., now president of Ferry Research and Development Laboratories in Cambridge, Wisconsin, sent a copy to Jenny. "Ruth and I were very provoked at Henry," Frank said. "We were going to write him but decided to wait until we talked with you." Jenny thanked her brother and wrote her other siblings as well as Parsons. Calling the hearing nothing more than harassment and nuisance, she erupted. "What are the communistic principles he [Cape] refers to? Brotherhood among all peoples? Peace in the world? Disarmament? Integration throughout the United States? Cooperation among people rather than competition? Socialized medicine? If these are some of his ideas of communistic principles, then it's about time the people of the U.S. woke up!" Craig wrote to Jenny's brother, Bob:

We did not use our guest ranch to recruit communists.

However, we were accused by a paid informer and perjurer of doing so. At that time—eight years ago—had I answered the questions put to me by the Senate Internal Security Committee, that committee would have taken the word of Matuso [*sic*], the perjurer, against mine. And there was no doubt in the mind of my attorney, or mine, that I would be tried for perjury and convicted by the testimony of Matuso.

A friend of ours, Clinton Jencks, was convicted upon Matuso's testimony and it took a Supreme Court decision to reverse the case, and that came only after Matuso admitted he did perjure himself. Later, M. was convicted of perjury and is still in prison.

It is hardly necessary to say so but Jenny doesn't sell records "inductive to communistic principles"—two people have repeated this lie—Henry Cape and the local priest in Taos.

Jenny was asked the same questions which the Committee asked me 8 years ago—and under all the circumstances her attorney felt she should do what I did. Although her inclination was to follow the thought of Dr. Albert Einstein and refuse to answer this committee at all.

The Committee, like the House Un-American Committee, is engaged in trying to destroy the reputations of people who believe in democracy and our Constitution—they, the Committee, are the real subversives.

Embarrassed, Sarah could never bring herself to speak of the incident, and she did not mention it in her annual post-festival report. She did, however, approach the FBI in 1961. In an apparent effort to gain increased financial support from government agencies, she inquired if J. Edgar Hoover might serve as honorary chairman of the 1961 festival. (He declined.) According to Jenny's FBI file, she also asked whether the group should encourage the use of folk singers such as Jenny Vincent and Pete Seeger who had appeared before Congressional Committees and refused to cooperate. Sarah referred to Jenny and Pete as "tremendously talented professionals in the folk singing field," and in view of their capabilities wondered if she had the duty or the right to exclude them from the program in 1961. She was advised that knowing the backgrounds of Vincent and Seeger she must "judge for herself whether they represent the best traditions of our Nation."

Knott must have been considerably shaken by the 1960 incident to make this token overture. In time, however, she regained her own judgment and her friendship with Jenny. By the 1965 festival in St. Petersburg, Florida, Jenny was once again a featured artist, representing New Mexican folk music with such songs as "La Casita en el Cerrito" ("The Little House on the Hill"). "Jenny Vincent," the festival program stated, "is one of the foremost singers of Spanish American folk songs in the Southwest. She has done much to bridge the gap between the Spanish and the Anglo and to portray the beauty of Hispanic heritage, usually overlooked in our country."

For her part Jenny never held Sarah personally responsible for what had taken place, but assumed she had been under pressure from a board of directors that capitulated to fear of controversy. Jenny understood that well. It was risky enough in these times to be labeled a union member or folk musician without also being from the atomic state of New Mexico. Throughout the entire hullabaloo no one seemed to notice that Jenny had come to New Mexico seven years before there even was a Los Alamos laboratory.

TEN

Movimientos

The twelve years from 1948 to 1960 had been a roller coaster of trials, triumphs, and turning points for Jenny. She had divorced her first husband and met and married her second. Her mother and stepfather had died. She had sung for a presidential campaign and on picket lines, actions for which she was vaunted by the people and vilified by the authorities. She continued to bring music to public schools and debuted at universities. She had closed her ranch and opened a music store. She released her first solo recording and formed a professional trio. She had been a heralded performer at national folk festivals and been dragged off their stage by a Senate investigating committee.

She also raised a son and saw him off to college, but Larry soon faced a turning point of his own. In the fall of 1959, before he finished his first semester at Colorado State College in Ft. Collins, he became utterly homesick. He wanted to drop out and return to San Cristobal.

It wasn't the first time Larry had been unhappy in school. After starting elementary school in Albuquerque, Larry Vincent (he had taken Craig's name) entered fourth grade in San Cristobal.

Blond, freckled, bespectacled, and speaking no Spanish, Larry was a prime target for taunting by his new peers. He soon complained to his mother that he was being discriminated against. "Larry," Jenny said, "what is the language of the school?" "English," he answered. "So who," she asked, "is being discriminated against?" Jenny encouraged Larry to pick up Spanish from other kids. "We told him to go ahead and learn the dirty words first," she says, laughing. "That's probably what they were using when they teased him anyway. He said they'll laugh at me, and I told him that the same kids who laugh at you now will end up being your teachers and friends."

Larry started out of necessity—*scalera* (ladder), for example, when he needed to rescue a softball from the school's flat roof—and he was persistent. Eventually he would become so thoroughly bilingual that today his English is faintly accented. He earned respect as well. One day, a classmate who rode a horse to school lassoed Larry with the intention of dragging him. Always a resourceful kid, Larry quickly whipped out a pocketknife and cut the rope.

The friendships he made during those years remain strong. His closest friend, Jose Leon Trujillo, remembers those school days with fondness and frequent laughter. "I stayed up at the ranch a lot, and Larry would come down and stay at our house," he says. "When you're kids, you can communicate even without language, but he was picking it up quickly. In the summer of '53 or '54 I went with Larry to the Wells summer place in Wisconsin. He said I'm not going unless Jose goes with me! I went for about two months, and all we did was speak Spanish together."

Jose Leon and Larry went through grade school and high school together. At Taos High School Larry got into agriculture, and it was there that he and Jose Leon began to play music seriously. Larry, of course, had been surrounded by music since before he could remember. He also received an introduction to the violin from his Grandpa Wells and the mandolin from Cleofes Vigil. In high school he started on guitar. Jenny loaned Jose Leon his first guitar—"a Gene Autry model." He and Larry and several friends formed the Aces, playing local dances and weddings as well as gigs in Colorado. "It was rock 'n' roll, you know?" says Jose Leon. "Drink a little beer, play a little music."

By the time he graduated from high school Larry had come full circle from his grade school misgivings. Now, in college in 1959, the kid who had been so tested by his peers in San Cristobal was homesick for them. Jenny and Craig took a calculated risk. They encouraged him to finish at least his first quarter and then decide whether or not he wanted to continue in college. Jenny also told him he couldn't just come back home to hang around with his friends.

The tactic worked. Larry finished his freshman year, then took a summer job with Craig's brother Bill planting trees in Olympia State Park in Washington. He listened when people other than his parents told him that if he wanted to get somewhere in forestry he needed a college degree. Larry began to alternate college terms with temporary jobs. He worked with the Forest Service in California's Shasta National Forest and for three seasons as a firefighter and smokejumper in Alaska, earning money to pay his own way through school.

Jenny came home from the Fulton Lewis uproar to receive a citation from the Taos Artists Association in honor of her contributions to the arts—and some hate mail. ("Here's a song for you," one postcard read: "When the Commies Come Back to San Cristobal.") It was only a few months before she and Craig were back in the public eye. "Vincent impressed with Cuba," read the *Taos News* headline in January 1961. "Craig Vincent of San Cristobal returned last week after a ten-day visit to Cuba, bringing a story which contradicts the one most Americans read in the newspapers and hear on radio and television." The article went on to quote Craig's glowing report of progress in Cuba. Craig had been one of a group of seventy-five to visit Cuba on a tour sponsored by the *National Guardian*. While sympathizers applauded his position, detractors thought him naive for accepting at face value what he had seen during a state-controlled tour. He and Jenny were controversial all over again.

That same year, 1961, also held a personal tragedy for Jenny. In her Salt Lake City home, Fran Wells DiSanti suddenly dropped dead of an apparent cerebral aneurysm. After marrying Joe DiSanti during the brief period she and Jenny lived in Albuquerque, Fran moved with him and her adopted daughter Wendy to Utah. In 1954 she gave birth to a son, Michael. A second son, Dimian (Dimi), followed in 1957. For Jenny, Fran's loss was insurmountable. No longer sisters-in-law, they had remained each other's best friend. Joe sent Jenny a memorial statement he had written: "She lived for others, her family, her friends, and the needs of society," he said. "She was simple and wise; she was quick to decry hypocrisy and quick to honor and respect the simple honesty in people.... She felt the vitality of living in conjunction with all others and sought, in her own individual way, to aid in the making of a better world."

In 1963 Jenny and Craig traveled to British Guiana (present-day Guyana) by way of Mexico and Venezuela. There, they visited Cheddi Jagan and his wife, the former Janet Rosenberg of Chicago. Born in British Guiana to parents of Indian descent, Jagan studied dentistry in the United States and returned to his native country steeped in Marxism and Gandhian nonviolence. In 1950 he helped form the People's Progressive Party and launched a long career in opposition to British and American imperialism. He would serve his country as president or premier on three different occasions. Jenny and Craig's itinerary was noted in detail by the FBI, and when they returned to the states via Los Angeles, Craig was detained at customs without explanation for an hour before being released.

That same year Jenny closed her Taos Music Center. The store had enjoyed an eight-year run, though it never really paid for itself. Her partner had been Joan Reno, whose husband, Phil, was one of Craig's closest friends. They knew each other from Colorado where Phil, a Marxist economist, was fired from his university teaching position. Joan, a pianist who studied at Julliard in New York, was apolitical and struggled when the Renos went underground. Phil spent two years in South America where, with Cheddi Jagan's encouragement, he wrote a book about British Guiana. When the Renos later showed up in Taos, Jenny brought Joan into the music center and Craig and Phil launched Taos Homes, a construction project designed to develop housing for low-income people. With the close of both the music store and the construction business, the Renos left Taos for Albuquerque. They would later divorce.

In 1966 Larry graduated with honors from Colorado State. Suddenly, he had to weigh his options. America was in deep in Vietnam and Larry, who opposed the war, considered conscientious objector status, Canada, or the Peace Corps. One of his professors encouraged him to apply for a Fulbright. For references on his application, Larry listed two professors and Cleofes Vigil. Cleofes brought his letter down for Craig to review, and Craig only corrected the spelling of one word. Cleofes's letter proved pivotal to the awards committee and Larry, to his own surprise, was granted a one-year fellowship to Venezuela. There he would earn a degree in forest ecology at the University of the Andes and subsequently become a faculty member, teaching entirely in Spanish. "All of this from a kid who originally didn't like to leave home!" Jenny says. "But he became completely independent and created a wonderful life in South America."

With Larry out on his own, Jenny and Craig were empty-nesters looking forward to doing some more traveling. In 1967, however, Joe DiSanti died. Years earlier Jenny and Fran had vowed to each other that should anything happen to either of them the other would take responsibility for the surviving children. In 1963, when Joe underwent surgery, Jenny had spent six weeks in Salt Lake City caring for Mike and Dimi. Now she had no hesitation about honoring her pledge to Fran. She and Craig formally adopted the two boys. She was fifty-four, and Craig sixty-three.

Fran and Joe DiSanti had been active in leftwing causes during the McCarthy period—the FBI pegged Joe as the head communist organizer in New Mexico at one point—and like many children of politically active parents Mike and Dimi had often been left with babysitters. Their parents had loved them, but when they arrived in San Cristobal they needed nurturing—and they were fighting, as nine-year-old Dimi tried to compete with his thirteen-year-old brother.

Michael would prove to be an exceptional student, graduating from Taos High School, the University of New Mexico, and going on to become an astronomer. Dimi struggled at first and ran with a fast crowd. Sent to Verde Valley School in Sedona, Arizona, he flourished and honed the musical skills he had begun to acquire from Jenny. "I taught him his first guitar chords," Jenny says, "but very soon he progressed far beyond me." Today, Dimi is a professional jazz guitarist based in Albuquerque. He and his brother have long since mended fences.

The boys' arrival in 1967 brought sudden changes to the Vincent household. Jenny and Craig gave up their bedroom so Mike and Dimi could have their own rooms and moved their bed into a library alcove. The personal dynamic also inevitably changed. "Craig was a good father to the boys," says Jenny, "but when I became a mother again I think it contributed to a cooling in our own relationship. We stayed close, but it seems like we lost some of our communication." Craig had never really been one to confide too much. Jenny suspects that he now may have begun to struggle with depression. "Our objectives had always been the same," she says, "but we were involved in different things." They began to lead somewhat parallel lives.

Reies López Tijerina, son of a poor Texas sharecropper, had been a migrant farm worker and a traveling revivalist by the time he arrived in New Mexico in the 1950s. There he founded the Alianza Federal de las Mercedes (the Federal Land Grant Alliance). Possessed of a fiery charisma and the oratorical skills to embellish his street smarts with visionary statements, Tijerina wanted the Alianza to confront one of the most incendiary issues in New Mexican history—the land grant controversy. The issue dated back to the 1848 Treaty of Guadalupe Hidalgo that ended the U.S.-Mexican War. The treaty took millions of acres of land away from Hispanic peoples whose families had originally received them from the Spanish and Mexican governments. The treaty's opponents considered it nothing more than one enormous land theft.

With Tijerina at its helm, the Alianza tapped into a well of resentment against what it said were years of racist policies and economic hardships perpetrated at the hands of Anglos. The Alianza held protests and marches and employed other tactics that Tijerina had learned from Bayard Rustin and Martin Luther King Jr. However, while the decade's most widely known Chicano rights organizer, César Chávez, consistently advocated nonviolence, Tijerina and his followers became increasingly militant.

The land grant controversy exploded onto the national consciousness in 1967 when Tijerina and about twenty of his followers stormed the Rio Arriba County courthouse to make a citizen's arrest on District Attorney Alfonso Sanchez, whom they accused of harassment. The "Corrido de Rio Arriba" memorialized the moment:

> *Ano de sesenta y siete*
> *cinco de junio fue el dia,*
> *hubo una revolucion*
> *alla por tierra Amarilla.*

> In the year of sixty-seven
> the fifth of June was the day,
> there was a revolution
> up there in Tierra Amarilla.

In the ensuing chaos several police officers were wounded or beaten and squad cars riddled with bullets. After a massive manhunt, during which police arrested Tijerina's pregnant wife, Tijerina turned himself in. He defended himself in court and, in a stunning verdict, was found innocent. He would later serve several years in prison stemming from other charges.

"A lot of the eastern writers who came in refused to believe that this was a serious protest," said Larry Callaway, a UPI reporter who was briefly held hostage during the raid. "They didn't understand the land issues, the water issues, the land grant situation. They tended, once again, to put that big grin on their face and treat the thing as a Western movie."

One year after the courthouse raid, Sanchez accused Tijerina of training guerrillas at a northern New Mexico ranch. Everybody knew where he meant. Craig Vincent called Sanchez's story malicious and false. (Jenny had repurchased the ranch in 1964; she and Craig were not living there but were renting it to various individuals and groups, including the Lama Foundation.) A police investigation found no evidence of such training.

The Alianza was part of a larger Mexican-American rights movement in the Southwest, and in 1968 another legendary *movimiento* leader visited the ranch. A former championship boxer and a leader of the Chicano rights group the Brown Berets, Rodolfo "Corky" Gonzales founded the Crusade for Justice in Denver and in his famous movement poem "I Am Joaquin" sounded the clarion call for action: "And in all the fertile farm lands / the barren plains / the mountain villages / smoke smeared cities / we start to MOVE!"

He came to San Cristobal with artist Bill Longeaux and Bill's wife, Enriqueta Vasquez, a writer and political activist. "Corky was urban and youth-oriented," says Vasquez, who is today a neighbor of Jenny's. "He talked about establishing a movement school—there had been a fire at Corky's school in Denver. So we came down to meet Jenny and Craig and talk about renting their ranch." The school did not materialize, but Vasquez would work closely with Craig on a number of political causes. "Craig used to come here for coffee all the time and bring people to talk politics," she says. "Corky once wrote a play which Craig passed on to Dalton Trumbo, but in the end no one could raise the financing to make it into a movie."

Craig had been talking with Reies Tijerina, who had become interested in working with senior citizens. Jenny and Craig agreed to rent the ranch to Tijerina for a two-week retreat. On Sunday, February 2, 1969, Tijerina announced that Jenny's ranch would be used as an Indo-Hispano cultural center. That night, the ranch burned down. Tijerina condemned the fire as further proof of a conspiracy to keep the Hispanic peoples from developing their culture, rights, and heritage. Craig, too, thought the incident simply too much of a coincidence to be anything but arson. "Mr. Tijerina made the announcement at two o'clock and the ranch was on fire by nine PM," he said. "Those are the facts."

Among the media reporting the facts was *El Grito del Norte*

(Cry of the North), a movimiento newspaper recently launched in Española by Elizabeth "Betita" Martinez and Beverly Axelrod. Martinez was one of only two Chicanas (the other was Maria Varela) working for the Student Nonviolent Coordinating Committee (SNCC) in New York when she came to New Mexico to scout out the possibility of starting a movement publication. There she met Axelrod, a civil rights attorney whose client list would include Eldridge Cleaver, Dennis Banks, and Jerry Rubin, as well as the Alianza. Martinez and Axelrod were careful not to appear as outsiders coming in to tell local people what to do. They spent a lot of time traveling to villages, talking with people about starting a newspaper and what they would want to see in it. They also met Craig and Jenny, who wrote them a check to help start *El Grito*. The Vincents later donated a car for the newspaper's use.

For five years *El Grito* covered national and international labor struggles, land issues, political prisoners, and everything else from black liberation to Mexican student protests, radical whites, and Cuba. Its staff comprised a remarkable group of predominantly female columnists, writers, photographers, and production workers, prominent among them Rini Templeton and Valentina Valdez well as Martinez and Vasquez.

No cause was ever determined for the fire that razed San Cristobal Valley Ranch. While Craig never accepted any explanation other than political arson, Jenny considered another possibility. At the time of the fire the hippie counterculture was booming in Taos County. Two days before the blaze, Jenny gave a ride to a young local man who had been hanging out with a group of hippies in an abandoned house in San Cristobal. He asked her for permission to use the ranch on Sundays for recreational purposes. When Jenny declined, saying she and Craig were preparing the ranch to be rented, the young man confessed that he and his friends already had been sneaking in on Sundays to use it. Jenny believes that this group built a fire in the large, second-story fireplace and that it accidentally got out of control. By the time firemen arrived on the scene, it was too late. "We could only stand there and watch it go," she says. "It was one of the saddest days of my life."

The sudden influx into of so many young people—as many as a thousand at the peak of the counterculture movement in the late '60s and early '70s lived in such now-legendary communes as New Buffalo, Morningstar, and the Hog Farm—would change Taos forever. At the time Taos Book Shop owner Claire Morrill wrote, "Our latest economic problem is our hippies. Ours seem mostly to be nonworking types who, learning that they can't live off the land, have found that so far, at least, they can live off the people, a viewpoint that Taos considers conspicuously unfair in a poverty area. . . . It is true that they shook up American values, gave them a much-needed aeration. Yet Taos had already discovered some of those better values: a simpler, more loosely structured pattern of life, a need for space, and less dependence on things relating to convenience, comfort, and pseudo prestige."

The clash of the freewheeling Anglo hippie culture and conservative Latino Catholicism led to many episodes of violence. Craig Vincent was one of those who tried to promote an atmosphere of tolerance. At one Chamber of Commerce meeting, during which members angrily denounced the hippies, Craig stood up. "Uh oh," someone said at the back of the room, "now we're going to get it." "Do you know," Craig said, "that if Kit Carson rode into town today, with his long hair and beard, that you would be saying the same things about him?" The room went silent.

Phaedra Greenwood, who came from the east and fell in love with Taos, understood that local residents had reason to feel invaded. Greenwood, who briefly lived at the Hog Farm and wrote for the counterculture newspaper *Fountain of Light*, later moved into town to become a freelance writer. "I have had Hispanic friends tell me that it was at that time that their own kids started using drugs," she says. "That may be true, but that was going to happen regardless. The problem was a lack of consciousness, not looking around at what was here. Once we started doing what the locals did—farming, raising animals, and so forth—they saw that we were all right."

Over time, hostilities tapered off. The hippie movement itself began to fade, victim to such factors as the continued presence of hard drugs, deteriorating living conditions at the communes, and unrelenting national media coverage that resulted in swarms of voyeurs and exploiters. Greenwood and those like her who stayed in Taos to create constructive lives represent the best of the counterculture, young people who were serious about finding an alternative to a life of material consumption.

For Jenny, the counterculture movement was a two-sided coin. "I have to say that it was very difficult for a while. Some of the hippies behaved in such an outlandish manner, not thinking about the culture they had moved into." She disdained the substance abuse and sexual excesses, particularly when flaunted in the face of her more traditional and conservative neighbors. On the other hand, as a lifelong communitarian, a witness to the Depression in the 1930s, a veteran of Progressive Party politics in the 1940s, and a victim of McCarthyism in the 1950s, Jenny observed these cultural dissenters with some interest. In their New Left politics she could see hints of the Old Left, as seen in this quote from *Fountain of Light* (1969): "Taos is a ruggedly beautiful place that offers us a chance to reacquaint ourselves with the Planet Earth." In their quest for a simpler life, she could recognize something of her own past. "When it all quieted down," she says, "it is amazing how many of them brought real talent to the community."

One leading member of the counterculture's communal movement was a young man who would come to occupy an important role in Jenny's life. Originally from Pittsburgh, where he developed a passion for jazz and avant-garde poetry, Rick Klein came to New Mexico by way of Paris, where he had been hanging out after college. He arrived looking for something new and with a small inheritance bought land in Arroyo Hondo, between Taos and San Cristobal, on which he and his friend Max Finstein founded the New Buffalo commune. Finstein had come from New York City with Rene Oppenheimer, who had heard Fulton Lewis's radio broadcast denouncing Jenny and decided she must meet the Vincents. Now Rene Rosequist, she would join Craig on a number of political projects.

"The land was going to be the provider, as the buffalo was the provider for the plains Indians," Klein once said. Of course, few members of the counterculture knew very much about living off the land, particularly in the challenging conditions in New Mexico. "Teachers appeared to us, though—the people from the Taos Pueblo. I don't know what it is about the people from the Taos Pueblo...they just have an incredible heart. They told me afterwards, 'Well, we saw you people, and we decided to take pity on you.' We were pretty pitiful.... But they knew that our hearts were in the right place, and their hearts were in the right place."

Klein acknowledges that the original idea for New Buffalo may have been naive, but it wielded a positive influence on a lot of people. An amazing number of people who came were really lost, he says, people from cities, people who were into drugs, but in New Mexico many found some values that had to do with the earth and with work and with other people. They clarified their ideas and simplified their lives. "The main truth that came out of the 1960s," Klein said, "is that we are all one. Nothing is separate."

ELEVEN

Keepers of the Flame

Throughout the turbulent sixties Jenny continued to perform with the Trio de Taos, sing in the public schools, and record local musicians. Taos Recordings and Publications followed its initial releases by Pete Concha with more records: *Taos Matachines Music* by Adolfo Fresquez and Tranquilino Lucero; *Taos Spanish Songs* by Meliton Trujillo; *Bailes de Taos* by Francisco Vallejos and Rafael Martinez, who performed as Los Charros; *Piezas Antiguas* by Los Charros; *Picuris Indian Songs* performed by Ramos Duran and Pat Martinez; and, in 1970, *Buenos Dias, Paloma Blanca: Five Alabados from Northern New Mexico* sung by Cleofes Vigil. TRP's final recording, *Piezas Antiguas* by Adolfo Fresquez and Tranquilino Lucero, would follow in 1975.

TRP also published its first book, a 1962 reissue of *Patrocinio Barela: Taos Wood Carver*, a celebration of the famed "primitive" sculptor who would die two years later in a fire in his ramshackle studio. The TRP edition contained the original book's photographs by Mildred Crews Tolbert and excerpts from interviews with Barela by Wendell Anderson set in the form of poetry by Judson Crews.

With these recordings Jenny, through TRP, firmly established herself as not only a collector and performer but a preservationist

133

helping to keep valuable and historic musical traditions alive. "Their recordings and books are on the sought-after list of most of the nation's art collectors and museums," the *Denver Post* reported in 1966. "Chances are that none of the records put out by the firm ever will make the top 20 list. But at least that many prominent museums are waiting for the next release."

DESTROY THE HIPPIES, spelled out in white tape across the side of a car, was one of the first sights the new arrival saw when he reached Taos in the spring of 1969. Having heard stories of a hippie El Dorado somewhere around Taos, this was not exactly what he had expected to see. But it was not the lure of the counterculture that drew the young John Nichols to the area. As sympathetic as he was to many aspects of the hippie movement, particularly its antiwar stance, he was attracted by New Mexico's resemblance to a colonial country, a place where political struggle could be focused as in other parts of the world.

Nichols had traveled through Central America, where he was appalled by U.S. complicity in the wretched conditions many peoples endured there, joined antiwar demonstrations at the Pentagon, studied Marx and Malcolm X, and read *El Grito del Norte*. Shortly after arriving in Taos he started writing for a short-lived muckraking journal called the *New Mexico Review*, with art direction and production assistance from Rini Templeton. When the review went bust in 1972, he began to produce a steady stream of fiction and nonfiction books, among them *The Sterile Cuckoo* and *The Milagro Beanfield War*.

Nichols began to attend public meetings on grassroots issues facing the Taos Valley and inevitably met Craig Vincent. "Here was this strange man who always sounded like the voice of reason," Nichols recalls. "He would say 'Let's work it out, let's explore all sides of the problem.' More than that, Craig seemed downright gentle in the midst of all these maelstroms gallivanting up and down the valley." They became collaborators in many causes, among them the U.S.-China friendship committee, opposition to the war in Vietnam, and protesting U.S. policy in Central America. Craig would also spearhead a short-lived political publication called *El Spirito del Norte*.

In 1969 Jenny participated in workshops at the Highlander Folk Center in Tennessee. Founded by Myles Horton, Highlander was a center for people working for social change, particularly known for its involvement with the Civil Rights movement, serving as a meeting place for students who would create the Student Non-Violent Coordinating Committee (SNCC) and the Southern Christian Leadership Conference (SCLC). It had also been burned out of its original location by local segregationists. There Jenny and a young Puerto Rican named Miguel Torres translated and added a new verse to "De Colores," a song that captures the essence of Jenny Vincent.

> *De colores, de colores se visten los campos*
>   *en la primavera,*
> *de colores, de colores son los pajaritos*
>   *que vienen de afuera.*
> *De colores, de colores es el arco iris*
>   *que vemos lucir;*
> *y por eso los grandes amores,*
>   *de muchos colores me gustan a mi,*
> *y por eso los grandes amores,*
>   *de mucho colores me gustan a mi.*

> De colores, many colors are all of the gardens and fields
>   in the springtime,
> de colores, many colors are all of the birds
>   flying in wingtime;
> de colores, many colors we see in the rainbow
>   shining above us,
> that's why the love that embraces all colors,
>   all races is greatest for me,
> that's why the love that embraces all colors,
>   all races is greatest for me.

That same year Tierra Amarilla's only doctor announced that he was selling his clinic and moving. This was catastrophic news for Rio Arriba County; proper health care now would be at least seventy-five miles away. Jenny and Craig had already helped the establishment of La Cooperativa, an agricultural cooperative in Tierra Amarilla. Now they threw their support behind the organization of La Clinica del Pueblo de Rio Arriba. With assistance as well from some of Craig's friends and political connections, La Clinica managed to raise the money for a downpayment. In September the clinic was burned by arsonists. "People were saying the co-op supporters were just a bunch of commies," says John Nichols.

The crime strengthened the resolve of those who supported the clinic. Tierra Amarilla became a consuming project for Craig. He worked closely with a determined group of volunteers, among them Maria Varela, Valentina Valdez, and Valentina's husband, Anselmo Tijerina, Reies Tijerina's brother. Craig helped establish the legal framework for a nonprofit corporation that could operate the clinic. "He was everything to us," Valdez says. "He helped us in so many ways. And with her devotion to music and bilingual education in the schools, Jenny was an inspiration."

"Craig looms very large in our lives," says Maria Varela. "He was funny, down to earth, and a great mentor. He gave us a sense of how something should operate. He was our organizational development person, watching over us to ensure that everything complied with the law. He gave structure to our passion, and we trusted him because we knew it was his passion, too."

Among La Clinica's supporters were several Albuquerque women, themselves no strangers to social movements, who operated as the Friends of the Cooperativa Agricola—Helayne Abrams, who was involved in the U.S.-China group; Floy Barrett, a veteran of the civil rights struggle in the South; and Dorie Bunting, head of the Albuquerque Center for Peace and Justice. All became Jenny's personal friends.

In the fall of 1970 Taos hosted a festival marking the fortieth anniversary of the death of D. H. Lawrence. The four-day conference drew four hundred participants from around the world and served to remind Jenny of her Lawrence trek thirty-five years earlier. Claire Morrill noted, "Except for Jenny Vincent and panelist Joe Foster, the Taos contingent of D.H.L.'s friends remained discreetly absent from this affair, though Brett came in to tell me, 'I don't want you to think I'm just being difficult. I'm just too old and too deaf.'" The festival also reunited Jenny with Enid Hilton, who had been living in California. Enid broke up the conference when she related the story of sneaking *Lady Chatterley's Lover* into England by stuffing copies into her clothes. "I already had plenty of bulges," she said, "so what were a few more?"

Two months after the Lawrence conference, President Richard Nixon signed legislation that returned to the Taos Pueblo its sacred Blue Lake and surrounding land. This was the culmination of a struggle that began in 1906, when the government took 50,000 acres from the pueblo for what would become Carson National Forest. Soon, roads were built into the wilderness and loggers, hunters, and campers began to show up. The government offered to purchase the land, but the Tiwa did not want dollars. They wanted their land. High up on Pueblo Peak (a.k.a. Taos Mountain), Blue Lake is sacred to the tribe not only as its source of water but, according to oral tradition, as the very waters from which the tribe was created.

In 1933 Congress granted the Indians a fifty-year special use permit. This did not prevent the Forest Service from allowing recreational use of the land. The pueblo attracted high-profile friends during its struggle, among them John Collier, Mabel Dodge Luhan, and writers Oliver La Farge and Frank Waters. Finally, a group of political heavyweights entered the fray, among them Secretary of the Interior Stuart Udall, his brother Senator Morris Udall, and Senators Clinton Anderson, Fred Harris, Barry Goldwater, Robert Kennedy, and Edward Kennedy. In *The Blue Lake Area*, a mid-sixties published appeal from Taos Pueblo, pueblo Governor Teofilo Romero said, "Now is the time for the United States Government to say clearly that the land belongs to us, even as we have always said that we belong to the land."

In 1969 tribal elder Paul Bernal testified before Congress: "In all of its programs the Forest Service proclaims the supremacy of man over nature. We find this viewpoint contradictory to the realities of the natural world and to the nature of conservation. Our tradition and our religion require people to adapt their lives and activities to our natural surroundings so that men and nature mutually support the life common to both. The idea that man must subdue nature and bend its processes to his purposes is repugnant to our people."

Craig and Jenny were among the local residents who supported the pueblo. Craig remained behind the scenes, knowing full well that his political reputation might do more harm than good. "I don't want to call it a secret committee," he later joked to artist John DePuy. Craig and his colleagues on this committee—among them Collier and Waters and Phil Reno—would meet with pueblo leaders to offer ideas and assistance. It was up to the pueblo to decide whether or not to use the ideas. Nobody was more overjoyed than Craig when Blue Lake was returned; he could only shake his head that it was Nixon who did it. When Enriqueta Vasquez later bought a book about the Blue Lake story, she was furious to find Craig mentioned only as "that communist." "I was so angry, after all of the work he put into that."

In the early 1970s two women, Peggy Nelson and Junella Haynes, arrived separately in Taos and became players in Craig's causes and close friends of Jenny. Fresh from law school in California, Nelson went to work for the Taos Community Law Service. As a law student she read the United States v. Clinton Jencks case, during which Craig was subpoenaed as a hostile witness. After meeting Craig, Nelson became involved in the local chapter of the U.S.-China People's Friendship Association, which Craig had helped found after attending the inaugural convention of the USCPFA in 1974. Nelson soon joined Craig, John Nichols, and others in regular political and policy discussions.

Nelson, who would go on to become a public defender and district judge, eventually bought a house in San Cristobal from the Vincents—Diego Arellano's original home. Nichols once said that Craig had great hope and enthusiasm and an endless curiosity about the doings of this planet. He saw to it that a number of local people visited China. Peggy Nelson was the first, followed by Frank Waters, Taos Mayor Bobby Duran, Enriqueta Vasquez, and Junella Haynes, among others. Neither Craig nor Jenny ever went, always deferring to others.

A native of Oklahoma, Haynes, who is part Cherokee, had been at the University of California-Berkeley during the Free Speech Movement. In 1971 she arrived in Taos to visit friends and ended up staying for several years. Haynes had already been to China when she became involved in the U.S.-China organization. With historian Roxanne Dunbar-Ortiz and Phil Reno, who was pursuing an advanced degree, Haynes helped establish the Native American Studies Program at the University of New Mexico. Now living in Silver City, Junella returns to San Cristobal frequently to visit Jenny.

The International Folk Music Council held its 1973 convention in France, during which Jenny was invited to deliver a paper on the role of folk music in education. Identifying herself as a singer of folk songs—as distinguished from an ethnic folk singer—who had devoted her musical energies and interests to promoting the use of indigenous folk songs and music in the schools of northern New Mexico, Jenny expressed her conviction that folklore in general, and folk music in particular, should be recognized as dynamic and exciting tools to be encouraged in our schools, "not only in New Mexico USA but in every corner of the world, and most especially where children are struggling for their own self-identity." She concluded her presentation with the following statement:

> I do not propose that folklore be taught in our schools as
> a specific discipline in the curriculum, but that it be used
> to enrich and vitalize the history and geography classes,
> the literature studies, that are already being taught.

I propose that folk songs and folk music be encouraged in all chorus and band programs.

Communication with the community in which the school is located could be meaningful through involving the folk artists of the area in the classroom. Through the application of folk music in this manner, the schools can help to expand the musical horizons, and the appreciation of cultural heritage of not only the students but also the rest of the community. In short, the sharing of folk song and music experiences can go a long way toward breaking down barriers that often exist in multi-cultural schools and communities.

In short, "breaking down barriers" is the key to everything Jenny believes about folk music. The lessons she had gleaned from a half century of hearing folk music and three decades of performing it, lessons begun in intuition that she now articulated, pointed to one conclusion: the value of international folk music, both in and out of the classroom, is that it unifies people at the same time that it opens them to other cultures. It is a concept rooted in community, a conviction that takes on larger significance when one realizes that Jenny considers all of us members of the same global community.

As a schoolchild Jenny had sung "Frere Jacques" in the fourth grade and learned "Jesus Loves Me" in Chinese from a group of missionaries visiting Winnetka. She felt the music opened the world to her. As an adult performer she had devoted herself to open-ing doors for others, be they public school children, war veter-ans, political campaigners, union members, college students, folk dance enthusiasts, people of many different languages. Folk music had given Jenny entrée into all of these worlds. In the end it comes down to education. She had personally witnessed the effect of folk music in schools, and was convinced that the exposure of people to other cultures at a young age might reduce the likelihood of con-flicts between cultures in the future.

During the 1970s Jenny was a frequent participant in regional folk festivals, from Idyllwild, California, to Fox Hollow in New York. At home she made several guest appearances on "Sandia Sounds," a public television folk music program broadcast from Albuquerque, and for a year and a half hosted a weekly, thirty-minute folk music program over KKIT radio in Taos.

In 1970 Taos Recordings and Publications released Cleofes Vigil's *Buenos Dias, Palomas Blancas: Five Alabados of Northern New Mexico*. Cleofes first received musical training in a Civilian Conservation Corps (CCC) camp during the Depression. In 1940 he returned to San Cristobal and married Frances Arellano, daughter of Juan Arellano, Diego Arellano's brother. That same year Juan B. Rael, a professor of modern languages at Stanford University who had grown up in Arroyo Hondo, recorded Luis Montoya and Ricardo Archuleta, members of the Penitente Brotherhood, in nearby Cerro singing *alabados*. From the Spanish *alabar*, to praise, the *alabados* are religious hymns or chants that came by way of Spain to New Mexico, where they are most often associated with the lay religious sect, Los Hermanos Penitentes. Cleofes likely was influenced by the Cerro recordings, the latter the source of Jenny's "El Tecolote."

A poet as well as a musician, Cleofes was quoted in the album's liner notes, "I like the music, naturally, but the words— there's a meaning in each and every verse of any *alabado*. Let me tell you why the poets and why the old-timers in these valleys of the Sangre de Cristo really adopted such a thing as the alabado. It's to make you think, so you could lead a better life with your neighbors, with your friends, as a brother."

In 1976, the country's bicentennial year, Jenny was scheduled to participate in a conference at Purdue University celebrating the life and work of Paul Robeson. But when Robeson died just before the event, the conference turned into a memorial for him, and Jenny was quickly enlisted by Earl Robinson to play the piano for a special tribute he had written.

━━◇━━

The musical highlight of the decade for Jenny was the 1977 release of *Musica para una Fiesta* by the Trio de Taos, an album containing fourteen songs. While the trio was known for its far-ranging repertoire, for this recording it limited its program to popular *piezas* of northern New Mexico including such signature pieces from the WPA collection as "Amor Ardiente" and "La Varsoviana." To the eleven instrumental numbers Jenny added vocals on "La Casita en el Cerrito," "El Dia de tu Santo," and "Chiu Chiu," the first two from the WPA archives and the third a folk song from Uruguay. Jack Loeffler produced the album for Jenny's Cantemos Records. Loeffler had a professional studio in Santa Fe, where he normally did all his production, but for the Trio he opted for the intimate acoustics of Hattie's living room.

Jenny wrote in the liner notes, "the Trio's inspiration has come from families and friends, to whom this album is dedicated, and from the many Taos folk dancers and the musicians in the area who have contributed their talents to what has become known in New Mexico as the Taos Sound."

"It's Hard to Sit Still When Listening to 'Taos Sound'" read a headline in the *Bennington* (Vermont) *Banner*, of all places. Reviewer Valerie Restivo raved about the record:

> Jenny Vincent is known for her recordings of Spanish children's songs, her spirited folk festival performances, her scholarship, and her pioneering work in the New Mexico schools teaching language and cross-cultural fellowship through music. In person, she radiates an enthusiasm and a delight few can resist. . . . the Taos Sound is a mingling of Spanish and Anglo cultures that emerged as a unique blend. Flores's guitar is solid; Trujillo's mandolin is spectacular. The familiar Vincent sound is there—the sweet accordion and the clear, sparkling soprano that reveals, never dominates, the music. The album comes with an insert offering lyrics, chords, and notes. Started by scholarly labels such as Folkways, this is a tradition I dearly love. It encourages

participatory rather than passive listening. *Musica para una Fiesta* is a guaranteed high and a good teaching record as well.

The success of the record contributed to a growing demand for the trio. Already staples at the annual Fiesta de Taos; the New Mexico State Fair in Albuquerque, where it won a prize for best presentation of New Mexico music; and such special events as the 350th anniversary of Taos celebration in 1965, the trio also performed at the dedication of the Rio Grande Gorge High Bridge, the opening of the Bicentennial Exhibit at Santa Fe's Museum of International Folk Art, and at the Harvest Festival at El Rancho de Las Golondrinas. One of the most rewarding trio gigs, from Jenny's standpoint, was providing music for Fandango, a seventh-grade folk dance group that learned dances from older members of the Taos community. One year the trio accompanied the group throughout northern New Mexico.

"Kids don't hear this music now," she later told writer Jim Sagel. "Today's music is designed to make money. It doesn't have the function that folk music once had, to provide news, stories, and entertainment. I think of myself as a catalyst. I've dedicated myself to emphasizing the importance of the folk music of our area."

All the time Jenny was busy with her musical activities and with the care of her two adopted sons, Craig continued his slate of social and political causes, all of which Jenny supported both personally and financially. The two were increasingly apart. Jenny remembered something Fran had told her years ago about her first husband, Fred Gunther. "When we were both working he would come home and the first thing he did was sit down and see what was on television. No 'How are you, how was your day.'" Jenny could now relate to that; she missed the intimacy she had shared. Larry suspects that Craig may have had other relationships, and had he been financially independent may have left the family altogether.

Sadly, Jenny recognized a pattern repeating itself. She had long suspected that money was part of what came between her and Dan; now she sensed a similar situation. Craig Vincent was a proud man, but neither the guest ranch nor Taos Homes had been profitable. His attempt with *El Crepusculo* was short-lived. His ownership of the Patio Restaurant (now the Alley Cantina) with another old friend, Harold Johnson, had been similarly brief, and their friendship ended acrimoniously.

In the early 1980s Craig took a risk in the stock market. The gamble proved disastrous. He lost a lot of money, both Jenny's and his own from previous sound investments. "Craig was normally a good investor," Jenny says, "but for some reason this time he went ahead against the advice of his financial adviser. I think it was that as much as anything else that turned him downhill," Jenny says. "I didn't talk with Larry and Mike and Dimi about it at the time, but I think that is when he started to give up."

That, and his health. Craig Vincent was dying. A chain smoker for half a century, he was succumbing to emphysema. His friends had seen it coming for some time. "He was the only man I knew who inhaled oxygen through a tube in his nose and smoked a cigarette at the same time," said John Nichols. One Fourth of July, Peggy Nelson was setting off some fireworks. She made sure that Craig was sitting far away because she feared his oxygen tank would blow while he continued to smoke. Of course Nichols and Nelson were not alone in either their concern for Craig or their inability to do something about it. Jenny herself felt the inevitability of the situation. She simply could not force him to do something he was unwilling to do.

Jenny remembers 1981 for two memorable events. She attended an American Folklore Society conference in Minneapolis, and while there she made a nostalgic return to Northfield, for the first time in many years, to visit her birthplace and her father's grave. On a more solemn note, that year she and Craig attended a memorial service for Phil Reno in Shiprock. Following the breakup of his marriage, Phil earned a master's degree at the University of New Mexico and became devoted to Navajo Community College, now Dine College, in Shiprock, where he taught and lived on the reservation. He wrote important books—*Mother Earth, Father Sky* and *Economic Development: Navajo Resources and Their Use*—and was beloved by his Indian colleagues. Everyone was shocked when, in 1981, he committed suicide.

The following year Craig received a civil libertarian award from the New Mexico chapter of the American Civil Liberties Union. In public he could still give off an air of assurance. Inwardly, he was suffering. The stock market debacle and his deteriorating health were leading him into bouts of depression. It had been Craig who reinvigorated Jenny after her first marriage, Craig who helped her shape much of her political life, Craig who had been husband, lover, friend, mentor, and playmate for thirty-five years. Now Jenny saw him slipping away, anguished that she could not prevent it, could not reach him.

But she did. For the last two years of his life, Craig was largely homebound. He kept up with news and current events on radio and television and he read constantly. "He had never really depended on me emotionally," says Jenny, "but during those two years I could see us come back together. We put the TV in his room, and he wanted me to sit there with him. I sat there for two years." Out of this severe—and final—test of their relationship, their union returned. Only in the last year of his life did he stop smoking, by then an irrelevant gesture. In 1984 a room at La Clinica was dedicated in his honor, but he was too sick to attend. Jenny and Larry stood in his place.

On July 2, 1985, Jenny had lunch with Peggy Nelson and another friend, Peggy Beck. When Jenny arrived home Craig said to her, "I think I should be in the hospital." She called an ambulance to take him to Holy Cross Hospital in Taos. At eight o'clock the next morning the phone rang, and a nurse asked Jenny if she had been having trouble waking Craig up. Jenny said only if he had taken a sleeping pill. In twenty minutes the nurse called back. "Jenny, carbon dioxide is taking over and his blood pressure is going down." Jenny drove to the hospital as quickly as she could. By ten o'clock Craig was gone.

A doctor told Jenny that if she hadn't been there they would have put Craig on a respirator, but they knew neither she nor he would have wanted that. "He went very peacefully," the doctor said. Craig Vincent was seventy-eight. Among the first people Jenny called was John Nichols. The next day, July 4, Nichols drove out to San Cristobal and under the towering willow trees beside the Vincent home he and Jenny sat and talked for a long time.

"The sun was rising over the ridge," Larry later wrote, as people arrived at Jenny's house for a memorial on July 11. Family, friends, and neighbors exchanged greetings and *abrazos*. A number of people gave testimonials to Craig, among them Enriqueta Vasquez, Pete Concha, and Frank Waters. Stan Steiner added a little humorous perspective, "otherwise Craig would seem like a saint from heaven." Finally, John Nichols addressed the crowd.

> [Craig] believed in the good possibilities for human destiny, and he never got cynical.... He understood that you just simply never give in...that no matter what the hardship, you work to get joy out of whatever you are doing. I have often wondered what is the most important thing I could pass on to my own children, hoping to make their lives a little easier, more fulfilled, and dignified. And I've come to the conclusion that it really boils down to just one thing: I would hope, by my deeds, by my work, and by the style and concerns of my own life that I could help generate in them a sense of caring for the entire earth beyond themselves and their own everyday problems.... That is a gift I would also somehow like to pass on to my children.... Because I think we do have a bright future, if we all work together for it. That is a gift that Craig has passed on to me.

At the conclusion of Nichols's remarks, Jenny and Larry sang two of Craig's favorite songs, "La Feria de las Flores" and "Mi Ranchito." Then everyone joined in on a spirited version of "This Land Is Your Land."

What a man he was! Jessie O'Connor wrote to Jenny. "A real ornament to the human race." As the tributes continued to come in, Jenny faced the toll that two years of physical inactivity had taken on her. "I didn't take care of myself," she says. "I didn't even walk, and the next thing I knew I couldn't." Arthroscopies came first, followed by two knee replacements, one new hip, a hysterectomy, cataracts, and foot problems. The lifelong sportswoman was no longer able to enjoy long walks without a cane, but her history of physical activity served her well as she recovered from these ailments.

The 1980s held still more passages for her. Her friend Myles Horton, founder of the Highlander Folk School in Tennessee, died, and Jenny went back east to attend the funeral. Juan Chacon, of the Salt of the Earth strike and film, passed away, and Jenny personally expressed her condolences to her friend Virginia Chacon, with whom she had stayed in touch. In 1986 Rini Templeton, who had remained close to Craig and Jenny after the demise of *El Crepusculo*, suddenly died at age fifty-one in Mexico City, where she had been helping earthquake victims. Hattie Trujillo suffered a stroke that restricted the use of her right hand; after thirty years the Trio de Taos disbanded. Nat Flores moved to El Paso.

At seventy-two, Jenny might have retired to her home to live out her days. Yet in good times or bad, Jenny has never cut herself a lot of slack. Despite her physical ailments, she was curious about what life now would throw her way. She did not have to wait long to find out.

TWELVE

Her Shining Presence

There is only one solution if old age is not to be an absurd parody of our former life, wrote Simone de Beauvoir, and that is to go on, "pursuing ends that give our existence a meaning—devotion to individuals, to groups or to causes, social, political, intellectual or creative work." At the end of the 1980s, Jenny was ready to go on— go on living, go on making music. And as had happened before in her life when she stood at a crossroads, a kindred spirit now entered her life who would inspire her to take the next step.

Kindred spirit, free spirit, disciplined musician: that is how Jenny describes Audrey Davis. They met in 1988, when both were part of the volunteer orchestra for a local production of "The Wizard of Oz." Though separated in age by thirty years, the two women took to each other immediately. Audrey had grown up just around the corner from the house in Concord, Massachusetts, where Jenny and Dan had lived many years ago. She began to study the violin at age four and by fourteen was performing with the Concord Community Orchestra, the Quincy Orchestra, and the New Hampshire Symphony. She later married, raised a family, divorced, moved to Colorado, and finally settled in Taos, where she married photographer Bill Davis. She earned certification to teach the Suzuki method of violin and became one of the busiest music teachers in northern New Mexico.

Following their work together on "The Wizard of Oz," Audrey invited Jenny to play backup piano for her violin students' annual recitals. For Jenny, these recitals were further proof of what she has believed since the 1940s when she began to sing and teach kids in public schools: "Children should have ear training and be encouraged to play whatever instrument they start out with. Let them pick out things by ear. After all, we talk for five years before we're ever given letters to read."

As she approached her eightieth birthday in 1993, Jenny of course moved more slowly but otherwise showed little sign of slowing down. She served several years as president of the Taos chapter of the American Association of Retired Persons (AARP), though retiring from music never entered her mind. And in 1991 she and Hattie were honored as Women of the Year by the Taos Chamber of Commerce.

In 1995 Jenny published *Bailes y Musica para una Fiesta* under her Cantemos Records imprint. Jenny compiled the book in collaboration with Ollie Mae Ray, a choreographer and professor of health, education, recreation, and dance. She dedicated it to Hattie Trujillo and Nat Flores, "and to their families and mine; to the teachers and students who have used our recording; and to the folk dancers and musicians in the Taos area."

According to Ray, the idea for the book was conceived back in the late 1970s, when the trio produced its only recording, *Musica para una Fiesta*, and was intended as a companion to the record. It also was a response to requests from students and other people in classes, workshops, and at fiestas where Jenny played who wanted some of her songs available in musical notation. In the book Jenny and Ollie Mae provide not only the music for fourteen traditional folk dance tunes but notes on the provenance of each song, lyrics where appropriate, an introduction to the development of folk dances in the area, and instructions for dances to accompany the songs—all in a spiral-bound format that makes it easy for teachers and musicians to use.

The book was a significant contribution to the preservation and promotion of music and dances that are under continuous threat of being lost in the era of modern, industrially produced mass music. "These dances and songs represent a selected spectrum to include the traditional dances and songs from this particular area of the Southwestern United States," Ray wrote in the preface. "The intent is to preserve the dances and the music that have become classics (traditional)." Jenny herself had first learned some of these dances in the 1940s from Mela Sedillo-Brewster, a professor at the University of New Mexico who taught folk dances to children at Jenny's ranch.

Ray, who wrote most of the text, also solicited testimonials from former teachers Guadalupe Baca-Vaughn, Delores Varela-Phillips, and Ruth Rael, in whose classrooms Jenny had volunteered her time over the years. All said that Jenny's gift of giving and helping made her loved and revered by students, parents, and teachers.

There are two centers of action in Jenny's house and both are round oak tables, one in the kitchen and one in the music room. One year after the book's publication, Phaedra Greenwood interviewed Jenny for the *Taos News* at the table in her spacious music room, with musical instruments everywhere and shelf after shelf of recordings and song books. Dominating the room is Jenny's piano, the Steinway that her mother gave her on the occasion of her first marriage.

Vincent lives alone now, in an old adobe in San Cristobal among huge cottonwood trees and willows more than 100 years old, with a splendid view out her kitchen window of the Sangre de Cristo mountains. "I think I notice things more now that I'm alone," she says, "the blue sky, the sunsets, the birds, the different seasons of the year." It's a quiet life, but at a moment's notice she might dust off the piano and play the old folk songs she has always loved.

The simpler pleasures—tracking the seasons, watching for the hummingbirds, orioles, even an indigo bunting at the feeders near her sunroom windows—had always brought her comfort, now perhaps more than ever. And she continued two pastimes to which she gives at least partial credit for her longevity and marvelous memory: daily physical exercises, even within her limited mobility, and the crossword puzzles, word games, and other mental play that she has enjoyed all her life.

The moment's notice that Greenwood alluded to followed soon after the publication of *Bailes y Musica para una Fiesta*. The book caught the eye and ear of Jenny's new friend, Audrey Davis. Not only did Audrey buy the book and start her students on some of the tunes, she approached Jenny about the possibility of their performing together. Audrey had not played the northern New Mexico music and WPA songs before meeting Jenny, but she quickly fell in love with them. Then another musician entered Jenny's life.

Among the physical therapists that helped Craig Vincent in his final years were Jenny's longtime friend Junella Haynes and a woman named Terry Klein. Terry's husband is the same Rick Klein who cofounded the New Buffalo commune and became one of the central figures in the Taos counterculture. Rick was also a drummer and a rhythm guitarist who regularly backed up fiddlers—among them his son, Chris, a student of Audrey's who would win several fiddling competitions. Rick did not know Jenny but he knew Audrey, and when he caught wind of the music she was playing with Jenny, he expressed interest.

They immediately hit it off as a trio. The first time they played together professionally was in 1998, at the eightieth birthday party for Mary Wheeler, a lifelong New Mexico resident and close friend of Jenny's. After playing at Mary's party, Rick immersed himself in the music that he was learning from Jenny, music that he, like Audrey, had heard off and on through the years but had never played. He couldn't get enough. Awed by Jenny's musicianship and encyclopedic knowledge of folk music, Rick once introduced the trio as "the Jenny Vincent Experience." He was alluding to the Jimi Hendrix Experience, a band Jenny did not know, but the reference seemed to fit. It described something out of the ordinary. When they played their first Wool Festival in Taos, the master of ceremonies asked for the group's name. Audrey's impromptu answer was, "Oh, we're the Jenny Vincent Trio." "Pete [Seeger] wrote me a letter teasing me about using my name for the trio," Jenny says. "I tried to convince him it happened quite by accident."

A new band was born; Jenny was back where she belonged, performing before live audiences. With each successive engagement the crowds in attendance began to show increasing respect for this woman who had, over many years, become an institution. It was a new level of recognition for someone who had been fighting the good fight for a long time, and who had in the process remained true to her artistic vision. As Jim Sagel had written years earlier, it has been half a century since Jenny, following the lead of D. H. Lawrence, was taken in by the beauty of New Mexico, "but in the ensuing years, she has given much of that beauty back."

Thrilled to be playing in a regular group again—she had been deeply saddened by the disbanding of Trio de Taos—Jenny made an unexpected discovery. Her singing voice was intact. The Trio de Taos had been a predominantly instrumental ensemble, so Jenny sang only occasionally. Now, in her eighties and re-energized by Audrey Davis and Rick Klein, she found that she still had good pitch and a strong voice, even if it was a full octave lower than her once clear soprano. Jenny subscribes to the old adage of use it or lose it. "When I realized that I could sing again, I started all over with daily vocal exercises," she says. "The truth is, my lower voice of today is much more appropriate to the northern New Mexico music than my soprano ever was."

Other strands of Jenny's life seemed to be coming together in the 1990s. At the Taos Talking Pictures series, she sat with Virginia Chacon to watch a screening of *Salt of the Earth* and share memories now a half-century old. At the end of the decade Jenny received a visit from Henry Foner, a New York labor legend and president of the Paul Robeson Foundation. Jenny had long known about Foner for his activities with the Veterans of the Abraham Lincoln Brigade. Foner and his wife were celebrating their golden anniversary traveling in the Southwest and they wanted to meet Jenny. A long time ago Foner had penned a leftist tune that Jenny liked titled "Song of the Pennies," and when the Foners took her out to dinner in Taos she surprised and delighted them by singing it at the dinner table.

In 2000 Jenny answered a letter from Agnes "Sis" Cunningham, an original member of the Almanac Singers and cofounder, with her late husband Gordon Friesen, of the important song magazine *Broadside*. Jenny praised Cunningham for her fortitude during difficult times: "I am sure your musical ability and activities were sources for your positive approach to life." Jenny could have been writing about herself. Now referring to herself with tongue in cheek as a folk music practitioner on call, Jenny's own fortitude and musical ability were breathing new excitement into her life.

That same year she and Audrey and Rick entered a recording studio operated by local musician John Archuleta. Everywhere they played, the question had been the same: "Do you have a CD?" It was time, Jenny thought, to be able to answer yes. For the album she dipped back into the WPA archives that she had unearthed over fifty years earlier. The trio played dozens of tunes, ultimately settling on thirteen instrumentals drawn from the archives. Released on Jenny's Cantemos Records label, the CD is called *Spanish American Dance Tunes of New Mexico: WPA 1936–1937*. Its front cover carries a historic photo by John Collier Jr. of the 1939 Fiesta de San Geronimo in Taos, while the back cover bears a Bill Davis portrait of the trio. The two photographs represented a full circle for Jenny, a nod to the original era of the songs she specialized in—as well as to the cultural preservation work of the Colliers—and a contemporary photograph to indicate the new activity in her life.

Jenny provided notes that underscored the worldwide reach of folk music. "La Varsoviana," for example: "Varsovia is the Spanish word for Warsaw, and it was danced in the courts of Poland, probably traveled to Mexico with Maximilian and Carlotta, vanished from Mexico with them, and came north to New Mexico, where it

is still a popular dance. It is also known as 'put your little foot.'"
And "La Chinche," the Spanish word for bed bug, is built on the
Scottish folk song melody "Comin' Through the Rye." As Valerie
Restivo wrote about the Trio de Taos album in 1977, it is hard to
keep still when listening to this CD. The result is a recording that
is archival in its content and effervescent in its liveliness. At age
eighty-seven, Jenny had a popular record on her hands.

Videotaping began weeks in advance, courtesy of Ricardo and
Emelinda Medina, Jenny's long-time next-door neighbors—and,
in Ricardo's case, a former student at San Cristobal Valley School.
As local residents came into the San Cristobal post office, where the
Medinas' daughter-in-law Winda is postmistress, they would sing or
say a Happy Birthday wish to Jenny. First up was Larry's lifelong
friend Jose Leon Trujillo: "Happy birthday to you, happy birthday
to you; happy birthday dear Jenny, happy birthday to you!" Slight
dramatic pause. "And ninety more!" Children waved crazily into the
camera lens, calling out, "Hi, Jenny! Hey, Jenny! Happy birthday!"

On April 22, 2003, Jenny marked her ninetieth year with a two-
part celebration. At her house Michael, Dimi, nieces, nephews, cous-
ins, and grandchildren gathered for a family reunion. Larry flew in
from Venezuela. Later, the village turned out en masse at its community center to honor Jenny, applaud when she cut an enormous cake,
and join her to play music. As the afternoon wore on, a line of dancers snaked out the door and around the grounds outside.

In 2003 the trio continued to make regular appearances in
New Mexico and Colorado. At Taos's Western Sky Cafe one night,
Jenny sang "God Bless America," which she has rewritten with her
own lyrics as "God Bless the Americas":

> God bless America, which one do you mean?
> Is it north, or south, or central in between?
> 'Cross the prairies, to the islands, to the Andes,
>   white with snow,

> God bless the Americas, and Mexico,
> Gold bless the Americas, and Mexico.
>
> God bless the Americas, which God do you mean?
> Is it your God, or my God, or a God that remains unseen?
> Is it the rain god, or the war god, or Allah, or the dove?
> Please bless the Americas with peace and love,
> Please bless the Americas with peace and love.

Jenny's version of the song reflects her conviction that "America" rightly refers to all of the Americas—North, Central, and South— and that no one's God should be blasphemed as an excuse for killing one's fellow human beings. It drew a standing ovation. The audience demanded she sing it again so they could sing along. It was Jenny in her role as Jenny Appleseed, continuing to carry the message that music is a medium that can remake the world.

In April 2004 Larry returned from Venezuela to be with his mother on her ninety-first birthday, after which they drove across the country, visiting friends and family along the way, to Poughkeepsie, New York, where Jenny attended her seventieth class reunion at Vassar.

One week after Jenny returned from her reunion, the Jenny Vincent Trio played to a standing-room-only audience in the Taos Inn. The show had all the feeling of a homecoming celebration. Many old friends were there, as well as a number of Taos's younger musicians. Looking tired at first, Jenny grew visibly more energetic as the evening went on. By their second set, she and Audrey and Rick were rousing the crowd with Spanish-American polkas and waltzes, Mexican mariachi music adapted to their three instruments, Russian and Yiddish wedding dances, and cowboy songs. People were dancing in whatever small space they could find.

"When we play people are dancing and having fun," says Audrey. "What more could you ask for? I am having a wonderful time and so is Rick. Jenny is really someone to look up to. She tells such wonderful stories—a different story and sings a different song every time we play. I still haven't heard enough."

As Jenny had done ever since she began performing, she encouraged people to sing along, to remove the distance between performer and audience. Finally, they closed with the haunting love song "Las Golondrinas" ("The Swallows"), which members of the audience had been requesting. As Audrey drew out the final note, the trio was met with a standing ovation. The crowd would have welcomed much more, but Jenny, Audrey, and Rick locked hands together. They were through for this night. They had been playing for nearly three hours.

If you were in the audience that night, you experienced the musical arc of the long and vibrant life of Deborah Jeannette Hill Wells Vincent. All of Jenny was there in the songs she sang and the stories she told. The five-year-old in Northfield hearing folk songs for the first time: she was there. So was the teenage Winnetka tomboy who picked out songs by ear on her mother's piano. The Vassar class composer was there. So was the newlywed in Heidelberg, learning the accordion, and the new arrival in New Mexico, playing the piano while Frieda Lawrence sang. The hospital volunteer who entertained convalescing war veterans was there, and so was the public school volunteer. The political songster on the presidential campaign and the union maid on the picket line—they were both there. The promoter of international folk song and the preservationist of Hispanic tradition: both were there. So was the singer of romantic love songs. They were all there that night, all in the ninety-one-year-old recently off the road.

Jenny waited until the instruments had been packed. She chatted with a one-hundred-year-old man in a wheelchair who had tapped his fingers appreciably throughout the performance. She waited until the final fans and friends approached her to say how much she and her music meant to them, to recall mutual friends or a nostalgic memory, to have her autograph a CD, or just to bask in her shining presence. After they drifted away, Jenny carefully pulled herself up with her walker and started down the long hallway to the parking lot behind the inn. Her blue eyes shone brightly.

If you were walking behind her within earshot, you overheard two themes typical of the post-performance Jenny—a no-nonsense self-appraisal of her performance segueing into plans for the future.

"I was a bit rusty starting out," she said, laughing at herself, "still tired from the trip. I think we hit our stride in the second set. Rick and Audrey were fired up, weren't they?" She paused. "We are excited about expanding our repertoire. Rick has more cowboy songs he likes and is learning some lullabies for his new grandson. Audrey and I want to add some more international music. We would like to record another CD, with a lot of different material on it. Let's see, we have the annual Trade Fair at the Hacienda Martinez coming up and Wool Festival in the fall..." And you continued to follow her down the hall and listen as her voice trailed off and she stepped out into the New Mexico night.

Postscript

2006

Late one bright October morning a friend was driving Jenny the thirty miles from San Cristobal to Costilla. The northernmost village in Taos County, Costilla abuts the Colorado state line where Wild Horse Mesa tapers off. Jenny had not made this drive for three years, since the last time her trio played in La Veta, and it had been even longer since she had sung as a volunteer in the local school. Today she was going back. She had been invited by Rio Costilla Elementary School to perform for the children during the school's annual *cosecha*, or harvest festival. As she rode north, past Questa and Cerro, where the Taos Valley opens up into a sweeping vista, she reflected on what had so far been an extraordinary year for her.

It began in January, when the University of New Mexico honored Jenny for "her lifelong commitment to cultural activism in New Mexico through the music and dance of its peoples." For Jenny, it was a moving and nostalgic return to the campus where she first performed in 1947. This time she and Audrey and Rick played to an audience that included many old friends as well as students who could have been the grandchildren of those people in the audience fifty-nine years earlier. In May the state Historic Preservation

Division tapped her for a Lifetime Achievement Award in recognition of her more than sixty years of efforts to preserve the cultural heritage of northern New Mexico through music and activism.

Her music remained front and center through the summer and into the fall as the trio performed at the Albuquerque Folk Festival, the Fiesta de Taos, and the Village of Arroyo Seco bicentennial celebration, among others. September held a special moment for Jenny. When Amy Goodman, of radio's "Democracy Now," came through Taos to benefit Cultural Energy, a nonprofit educational radio station in Taos County, the station's Robin Collier asked Jenny, Audrey, and Rick to open the program with music. It was an extraordinary, spontaneous moment when Goodman crouched before Jenny with a handheld microphone to record her singing "God Bless the Americas," which received a standing ovation.

So there was much to reflect on as Jenny rode toward Costilla. What she did not know was that the *Taos News* had been planning for months to name her Citizen of the Year, a surprise they would spring on her in another two weeks. What she did know, and was pleased about, was the pending release of the trio's new CD, *Under the Western Sky*. It captures a rousing 2003 show at Taos's Western Sky Café. The audience that night was wildly responsive, so much so that the trio initially hesitated to release the recording. Eventually Tony Isaacs of Indian House Records, who had taped the original show, performed a masterful job of reducing the crowd noise, enough so that Jenny and Audrey and Rick agreed to release it.

The album comprises seventeen songs showcasing the trio's signature mix of New Mexican and Mexican waltzes, polkas, schottishes, and such favorites as "Mi Ranchito" and "Las Golondrinas." A few surprise bonuses from the live show are "A la Guerra Me Llegan Mi Madrecita" ("To the War They Are Taking Me Mother Dear"), which Jenny sang in 1945 to veterans convalescing in hospitals, her own "God Bless the Americas," and an exquisite, closing rendition of "Home Sweet Home." As with the Trio de Taos and previous Jenny Vincent Trio recordings, there is plenty of music for dancing, and with Jenny's vocals and commentary it captures the effervescence of her current live performances.

It captures, too, the themes for which she was applauded in her recent honors: art and activism.

Jenny Vincent—musician, activist. The former goes without saying, but the latter requires a broader reading of the word than is often understood. It does not begin and end with politics. Jenny's activism is a wider canvas. Music is her medium, and human rights and cultural preservation are her objectives. She is her own best example of what she said at that music conference in France years earlier: Exposure to international folk music can unite people at the same time that it opens them to other cultures. The more we open ourselves to other cultures, the less likely we are to enter into conflicts with those cultures.

The message of her music across cultures and generations was evident again at the elementary school in Costilla. It is a small school, with fewer than fifty students, precisely the kind of public school to which Jenny had devoted so much time over so many years. Sitting in a cafeteria room, enjoying a holiday potluck lunch with children, parents, and teachers, she smiled broadly. "I haven't been in this situation for a long time." She had not sung for schoolchildren in years, but as she later settled into a chair in the gymnasium and searched her mind for what to play, the songs returned to her as if no time had passed, particularly when one woman approached her and said that she had heard Jenny a long time ago, when she had been a student at the Fish Hatchery School, one of Jenny's regular volunteer rounds.

Jenny started with "Mi Chacra" ("My Farm"), an animal song from Argentina that she had recorded exactly sixty years ago on her first solo LP, *Spanish American Children's Songs*. In an instant the kids had joined her in the song, barking like dogs, braying like burros, and clucking like chickens. Jenny was reminding yet a new generation of their heritage. For her, every new generation carries with it the potential for a better world. The children of the world shall save the world. By the time she concluded her performance, parents and teachers had joined the kids in singing: "And that's why the love that embraces all colors, all races is greatest for me." It was "De Colores." It was the song of Jenny Vincent.

Sources

The primary source for this book is the series of interviews my wife and I conducted with Jenny Vincent. For the better part of two years, Jenny patiently answered our questions and shared with us diaries, correspondence, photographs, and other papers. At no time did she ask for manuscript approval, though I shared portions of it with her to ensure accuracy. I have not acknowledged her further in the notes that follow, but of course her presence should be assumed at all times.

Vital to the book was the unpublished diary of Jenny's mother, Deborah Sayles Hill Ferry, which she recorded from 1902 through 1948. The typewritten copy in Jenny's possession was prepared by Beverly Bosie-Cossart for Frank Ferry Jr. In addition, I examined a representative portion of Jenny's FBI file under the Freedom of Information Act, request No. 1005209-001. For author's interviews, see the Acknowledgments.

BOOKS

Baker, Ellen. *Salt of the Earth: Women, the Mine, Mill and Smelter Workers Union, and the Hollywood Blacklist in Grant County, New Mexico 1941–1953*. Madison: University of Wisconsin, 1999 (unpublished dissertation).

Cahalan, James M. *Edward Abbey: A Life*. Tucson: University of Arizona Press, 2003.

Culver, John C., and John Hyde. *American Dreamer: The Life and Times of Henry Wallace*. New York: Norton, 2000.

Dunaway, David. *How Can I Keep from Singing: Pete Seeger*. New York: Da Capo, 1990.

Gardner, Richard. *Grito! Reies Tijerina and the New Mexico Land Grant War of 1967*. New York: Harper & Row, 1970.

Geyer, Nancy. *The Vision of Perry Dunlap Smith*. Winnetka, Ill.: North Shore Country Day School, n.d.

Goldman, Eric F. *The Crucial Decade – And After: America 1945–1960*. New York: Vintage, 1960.

Gonzales-Berry, Erlinda. "Which Language Will Our Children Speak: The Spanish Language and Public Education Policy in New Mexico, 1890–1930." In *The Contested Homeland: A Chicano History of New Mexico*, edited by Berry and David R. Maciel. Albuquerque: University of New Mexico Press, 2000.

Jennings, Peter, and Todd Brewster. *The Century*. New York: Doubleday, 1998.

Keltz, Iris. *Scrapbook of a Taos Hippie: Tribal Tales from the Heart of a Cultural Revolution*. El Paso: Cinco Puntos Press, 2000.

Klein, Joe. *Woody Guthrie: A Life*. New York: Delta/Random House, 1980.

Lamadrid, Enrique R., consultant. *Nuevo Mexico: Hasta Cuando?* Albuquerque: National Hispanic Cultural Center in conjunction with the Smithsonian Institution, Albuquerque Museum, and University of New Mexico Chicano Studies Program, 2004.

Law, Lisa. *Interviews with Icons*, Santa Fe: Lumen Books, 1999.

Lichtman, Robert M., and Ronald D. Cohen. *Deadly Farce: Harvey Matusow and the Informer System in the McCarthy Era*. Urbana: University of Illinois Press, 2004.

Lieberman, Robbie. *My Song Is My Weapon: People's Songs, American Communism, and the Politics of Culture 1930–1950.* Urbana: University of Illinois Press, 1989.

Loeffler, Jack, Katherine Loeffler, and Enrique R. Lamadrid. *La Musica de los Viejitos: Hispano Folk Music of the Rio Grande del Norte.* Albuquerque: University of New Mexico Press, 1999.

Maddox, Brenda. *D.H. Lawrence: Story of a Marriage.* New York: Simon and Schuster, 1994.

Matusow, Harvey. *False Witness.* New York: Cameron & Kahn, 1955.

Morrill, Claire. *A Taos Mosaic: Portrait of a New Mexico Village.* Albuquerque: University of New Mexico Press, 1973.

Pearson, Drew. *Diaries 1949–1959.* New York: Holt, Rinehart and Winston, 1959.

Romero, Teofilo, et al. *The Blue Lake Area: An Appeal from Taos Pueblo.* N.p, n.d.

Schrecker, Ellen. *Many Are the Crimes: McCarthyism in America.* Boston: Little, Brown, 1998.

Seeger, Pete, and Bob Reiser. *Everybody Says Freedom.* New York: Norton, 1989.

Squires, Michael. *D.H. Lawrence Manuscripts: The Correspondence of Frieda Lawrence, Jake Zeitlin, and Others.* New York: Palgrave Macmillan, 1991.

Squires, Michael, and Lynn K. Talbot. *Living at the Edge.* Madison: University of Wisconsin Press, 2002.

Steiner, Stan. *La Raza: The Mexican Americans.* New York: Harper & Row, 1970.

Wells, Harry K. *David Herbert Lawrence: Poet of Organism.* Harvard University, 1934, unpublished dissertation.

INTERVIEWS, ONLINE SITES, AND PERIODICALS

Adams, David. *The American Peace Movements*, www.culture-of-peace.info/apm. September 2004.

Dimond, Ted. Interview with Rick Klein, KTAO-FM radio, Taos, N.M., 2003.

Dimond, Ted. Interview with Jenny Vincent, KTAO-FM radio, Taos, N.M., April 2003.

DePuy, John, and David Bertelsen. Unpublished interview with Craig and Jenny Vincent, San Cristobal, N.M., May 1980.

El Crepusculo, XI, 31-XII, 9. Taos: July 30, 1959– February 25, 1960.

"Frank Farwell Ferry 1878–1948." *Lake Forest Academy Alumni Spectator* 10, 1 (March 1948).

Greenwood, Phaedra. "A Song of Life with Jenny Vincent." *The Taos News*, January 25, 1996.

"In Memory of Fred Burnett Hill." *Carleton College News Bulletin* 1, 4 (February 1919).

Jackson, Bruce. "Harvey Matusow: Death of a Snitch." *CounterPunch*, February 20, 2002, file://untitled.matusow.htm.

Kaufman, Susanna. "Turning Points." Undated, unpublished interview with Jenny Vincent.

Malmgren, Peter, and Lucy Collier. Unpublished interview with Jenny Vincent, June 21, 1998.

Martinez, Elizabeth 'Betita.' "A View from New Mexico: Recollections of the *Movimiento* Left." *Monthly Review*, July–August 2002.

Maxwell, William. "Musician Jenny Vincent Instrumental in 1951 Mine Strike." *The Taos News*, March 13–19, 2003, B13.

"New Mexico's Memory of Land: The Legacy of Tijerina." Program no. 584, written and produced for Latino USA by Adam Saytanides, June 18, 2004.

Nott, Robert. "The Song of Jenny Vincent: Still Singing But Not to the Feds." *The Santa Fe New Mexican PASATIEMPO*, February 21–27, 2003, 38–39.

———. "At the Heart of the Matter: The Strike Against Empire Zinc." *The Santa Fe New Mexican PASATIEMPO*, February 21–27, 2003, 34–36.

Randall, Teri Thomson. "Making 'Salt of the Earth': Shaping Life into Art." *The Santa Fe New Mexican PASATIEMPO*, February 21–27, 2003, 24–30.

Rosales, Glen. "Musician Uses Spanish Folk Tunes to Express Herself." *The Albuquerque Journal*, July 2002, 14.

Sagel, Jim. "Jenny's Music: Her Songs Play Part in Preserving History." *The Albuquerque Journal*, September 25, 1982, C-4.

Steiner, Stan. "The Old Days." Unpublished interview with Jenny Vincent, 1977.

Steiner, Vera. Undated, unpublished interview with Jenny Vincent.

Taos Blue Lake, www.sacredland.org/historical_sites_pages /taos_blue_lake.html. September 2004.

PHOTOGRAPHS

Unless otherwise indicated, all photographs are from the archive of Jenny Vincent.

JENNY VINCENT DISCOGRAPHY

The Jenny Vincent Trio. *Under the Western Sky*, compact disc, San Cristobal, NM: Cantemos Records, 2006. Jenny Vincent, accordion and vocals; Audrey Davis, violin; Rick Klein, guitar.

The Jenny Vincent Trio. *Spanish American Dance Tunes of New Mexico: W.P.A. 1936–1937*, compact disc. San Cristobal: Cantemos Records, 2000. Jenny Vincent, accordion; Audrey Davis, violin; Rick Klein, guitar.

Trio de Taos. *Musica para una Fiesta*, cassette, San Cristobal, NM: Cantemos Records, 1977. Jenny Vincent, accordion and vocals (English and Spanish); Hattie Trujillo, mandolin; Nat Flores, guitar. Reissued 2004 on compact disc.

Vincent, Jenny. *God Bless the Americas*, compact disc single, San Cristobal, N.M.: Cantemos Records, 2006.

Vincent, Jenny. *Spanish Folk Songs of the Americas*, LP, San Cristobal, N.M.: Cantemos Records, 1956. Jenny Vincent, guitar and vocals (English and Spanish).

Vincent, Jenny. *Spanish American Children's Songs*, cassette, San Cristobal, N.M.: Cantemos Records, 1956. Jenny Vincent, guitar and vocals (English and Spanish). Reissued 2005 on compact disc.

Index